Computer-Assisted Language Learning: Concepts, Contexts and Practices

Computer-Assisted Language Learning: Concepts, Contexts and Practices

Edited by Jeong-Bae Son

iUniverse, Inc.
New York Lincoln Shanghai

Computer-Assisted Language Learning: Concepts, Contexts and Practices

All Rights Reserved © 2004 by APACALL

No part of this book may be reproduced or transmitted in any form or by any means, graphic, electronic, or mechanical, including photocopying, recording, taping, or by any information storage retrieval system, without the written permission of the publisher.

iUniverse, Inc.

For information address:
iUniverse, Inc.
2021 Pine Lake Road, Suite 100
Lincoln, NE 68512
www.iuniverse.com

The opinions expressed by the authors in this book are not necessarily those of the Asia-Pacific Association for Computer-Assisted Language Learning (APACALL: http://www.apacall.org/).

ISBN: 0-595-33126-2

Printed in the United States of America

Contents

List of Contributors vii
Series editor's preface ix
Preface xi

Chapter 1 Technology-enhanced language learning environments: A rhizomatic approach 1
Andrew Lian

Chapter 2 Narizoma: Critical pedagogy in practice 21
Ania Lian, Debbie Dolan, Grazia Scotellaro and Andrew Lian

Chapter 3 MOO virtual worlds in CMC-based CALL: Defining an agenda for future research 39
Mark Peterson

Chapter 4 CALL initiatives and the Korean cultural learning context 59
David Kent

Chapter 5 Language teacher trainees as multimedia designers: Voices from a CALL classroom 83
Arif Altun

Chapter 6 Teacher development in e-learning environments 107
Jeong-Bae Son

CHAPTER 7   Using text chat to improve willingness to
             communicate..................................123
   Lily K.L. Compton

CHAPTER 8   Making feedback last: An integrated approach to
             feedback in language learning 145
   Felicia Zhang

CHAPTER 9   Different learners and different feedback:
             Development of a computer-based essay marking
             system for ESL learners in Malaysia............165
   Saadiyah Darus, Supyan Hussin and Siti Hamin Stapa

Contributors

Arif Altun, Nigde University, Turkey

Lily K.L. Compton, Iowa State University, USA

Saadiyah Darus, Universiti Kebangsaan Malaysia, Malaysia

Debbie Dolan, University of Canberra, Australia

Supyan Hussin, Universiti Kebangsaan Malaysia, Malaysia

David Kent, Inha University, Korea

Andrew Lian, Rice University, USA

Ania Lian, Critical Pedagogy and Technology Consultants Pty Ltd, Australia

Mark Peterson, Tokyo University of Foreign Studies, Japan

Grazia Scotellaro, University of Canberra, Australia

Jeong-Bae Son, University of Southern Queensland, Australia

Siti Hamin Stapa, Universiti Kebangsaan Malaysia, Malaysia

Felicia Zhang, University of Canberra, Australia

Series editor's preface

The Asia-Pacific Association for Computer-Assisted Language Learning (APAC-ALL) is an online association established for language professionals working with computer-assisted language learning (CALL). Its Book Series thus covers a wide range of issues in CALL and offers opportunities for CALL researchers and practitioners to engage in research and discussion on their areas of interest.

This book is an examination of important issues associated with the application of CALL in language teaching and language teacher education. It offers insights into the questions of how CALL can be developed and used to improve teaching and how learners perceive and evaluate the value of their learning experience in CALL environments. It is a valuable contribution to CALL communities and stands out well as the first volume of the APACALL Book Series.

Jeong-Bae Son

Preface

This book explores various facets of computer-assisted language learning (CALL) and presents the findings of recent work in CALL that are of direct relevance to second language teaching and learning. It addresses issues such as the creation of online learning environments and systems, the importance of cultural contexts, the roles of language teachers, the use of computer-mediated communication (CMC) in teacher development, the impact of interaction and collaboration in CMC environments on second language development and the study of feedback on learners' pronunciation and writing. This volume reflects the diversity of CALL research and practice in a constructive way and provides a valuable resource for applied linguists, researchers, language teachers and teacher trainers.

The book includes nine chapters describing and discussing a range of CALL concepts, contexts and practices with current technologies of networking, multimedia and hypermedia. Chapter 1 introduces an intellectual framework for language teaching and describes a learning system that provides learner support and language at work in realistic settings through networked databases of multimedia materials. Chapter 2 deals with collaborative aspects of a Web-based educational environment. Chapter 3 reviews literature on multi-user object-oriented domains (MOOs) and examines the application of MOOs in CALL. Chapter 4 focuses on the relationship between the implementation of CALL and the Korean cultural learning context. Chapter 5 looks into English as a second/foreign language (ESL/EFL) pre-service teachers' meaning construction processes in a multimedia design task. Chapter 6 explores how CMC fosters teacher development in terms of communication, collaboration and reflection. Chapter 7 discusses the impact of online text chats on learners' willingness to communicate and self-confidence. Chapter 8 examines the use of a speech analysis tool offering audio and visual feedback. Chapter 9 investigates users' needs and expectations of computer-based essay marking systems with a focus on feedback on ESL students' essays.

In putting together this refereed volume, a collaborative effort has been made. I am grateful to the authors whose work appears in this book. I am also grateful to the reviewers of the manuscripts, David Ingram, Byungmin Lee, Andrew Lian, Shirley O'Neill, Mark Peterson and Marta Skrbis. I thank Critical Pedagogy and Technology Consultants Pty Ltd for helping to bring this book into the APAC-

ALL Book Series. I would also like thank my family, Minjung, Kyu-Sup and Kyu-Yeon for their love and support during the production of this book.

Jeong-Bae Son
Centre for Language Learning and Teaching
University of Southern Queensland
June 2004

1

Technology-enhanced language learning environments: A rhizomatic approach

Andrew Lian

Abstract

Theoretical models for language learning based on postmodern thinking are currently under development. These models argue for the development of learning systems which identify the process of (language) learning as a process of personal/individual meaning-making. This chapter describes progress achieved so far in one such model. This in turn forms the intellectual framework for an experimental technology-based environment designed to enable language learners to develop their meaning-making mechanisms by providing opportunities to confront, contrast and contest their understandings with examples of the foreign language at work. It intends to achieve this objective, in part, through the provision of support and help systems based on an infrastructure consisting of potentially large remote networked databases of multimedia materials showing language at work in realistic settings. The databases are complemented by systems designed to defeat the learners' perceptual systems. A proof of concept system will be described as will example applications. The strength of the system lies not only in each of its parts but particularly in the high level of connectivity between its parts: essentially a rhizomatic approach. Navigating through the system will enable learners to generate internal representations of the phenomena of the language which is being observed leading to more effective understandings of language at work.

Introduction

This chapter describes the development of a technology-enhanced foreign/second language learning framework and some aspects of its implementation. The chapter consists of three mutually referential parts which correspond to the three requirements necessary for any teaching/learning environment or structure: a guiding intellectual framework; an operational space (either physical or conceptual); and support structures and associated conceptual and physical tools.

Intellectual framework

While it is recognised that the focus of contributions in this book is necessarily on interesting *applications* of technology, the importance of the over-arching intellectual framework cannot be under-estimated.

The intellectual framework which informs this work finds its origins in the works of Petar Guberina (Guberina, 1976, 1972; Renard, 1978), a Croatian psycholinguistic and postmodern scholar *avant la lettre* who had been working on problems of perception with hearing-impaired people as well as people with normal hearing. His work in the area is based on what he called the verbo-tonal theory of perception. This theory which has tended to be overlooked or misunderstood in Anglo-American literature of applied linguistics provides us with interesting ways of thinking about perception and learning in general. Of particular interest in our context is Guberina's notion that deafness can be thought of not so much as a deficit caused by a physical defect but as ways of organising the world which are *different* from those which have been learnt by those who are not deaf. Keeping this principle in mind will enable the reader better to understand the development of the characteristics of the intellectual framework to be summarised below.

Guberina's work, while offering a crucial starting point for reflection in this and other papers (e.g. Lian & Lian, 1997) has subsequently been augmented, refined and reframed through application of the thinking of Pierre Bourdieu (1991; 1995), Jacques Derrida (1982), Anne Freadman (1994), Craig Calhoun (2000) and Ania Lian, et al. (2004).

Theoretical framework

Major characteristics of the framework used here have been established following an intellectual journey back to the basic principles not only of (language) learning, but of action in the world. Guiding the development of this process was the desire to arrive at a set of high-level coherent solutions for (language) teaching and learning, not merely a set of techniques.

In order to respond to that requirement, a question was formulated to help provide the starting-point for investigation. That question is: "How do we make sense of the world?" This is not a philosophical question such as "Why have we been put on this planet?" It is a much more concrete question with impact on every moment of our lives and it can be reformulated variously into: "What did this person say?" (for what we might call language—this will be recognised as an obvious example of attempted meaning-making) or into something common-sensically less obvious such as: "How do I not bump into other people as I walk down the street in Paris?" (sense has to be made of the situation in order to be able to go from point A to point B. If what is happening on the street is not understood and adjusted to, then moving forward will be impossible—not with safety at any rate and certainly with little popularity with passers-by). As we go about our daily activities, we are constantly engaging with complex multi-senso-rial information which we relate to our internal systems. In other words, we all constantly need to generate understandings in order to be able to act at all during each and every moment and every context of our daily lives. This is part of the human condition. The act of learning is no different. In order to learn, we have to make sense of what is happening: we generate meanings. We are essentially sense-making creatures.

Other aspects of the framework

Space does not allow detailed development of the consequences of the above, but they can be summarised in the points below.

a. Meaning is never found but constructed internally by each individual according to personal representational and logical systems which are the product of the individual's past. Ultimately, the act of understanding is always individual but shaped by the practices of society in interaction with us. It is constructed internally through a process of convergence from multi-channel experience and feedback: "A thing or idea seems meaningful only when we have several different ways to represent it—different perspectives and different associations. [...] In other words, we can 'think' about it. [...] So something has a "meaning" only when it has a few; if we understood something just one way, we would not understand it at all. That is why the seekers of the "real" meanings never find them." (Minsky, 1981).

b. We perceive the world and make sense of it essentially through the filter of our personal logical and representational systems, i.e. through the "filter" of our past (Bourdieu, 1995, p. 60). Paradoxically, these systems both help us to make sense of the world and limit our range of understandings. We never perceive the world directly (be it the perception of an individual sound or that of a complex human interaction). All we can ever access are perceptions and inferred meanings and, at a profound level, each individual's perceptions and meanings will be different from everyone else's though shaped by society as it interacts with us.

c. To learn implies an act of comprehension which challenges the learner's personal representational and logical systems i.e. which challenges their past. Learning is an act which brings into the learner's logical and representational systems that which had previously been excluded (unconsciously) by them. In a sense, it is an act of violence (in the sense of violating the regularities inferred by the individual on the basis of the past).

d. The act of comprehension can be thought of as an act requiring individuals to confront, contrast and contest their understandings and beliefs against the complexity of events unfolding around them, be they linguistic or non-linguistic events (Lian, 2000).

e. It is arguable that all of life is systematic and that all systems, however seemingly remote from one another, appear to be intertwined and mutually reinforcing. In our context, this applies particularly, but not exclusively, to semiotic systems. The thing to which we commonly refer in a common sense way as "language" is just one of the many intertwined systems that we need to manage and there is no doubt of its intertwining with others. An interesting example is the case of grammar and intonation. When grammar breaks down, the brain actually generates its own intonation patterns in order to compensate for the deficit (Herrmann, 2003).

f. A corollary to the above is that even if "language" were to be the primary focus, then the learning of "language" cannot be *only* about the learning of "language". It necessarily involves other systems which must be made to work in synchrony with "language": "we would say that any language developed by human society can be learned by the members of another human society, and that this learning is possible both because of the redundancy, which provides for a whole range of individual differences in sensory modalities, memory and intelligence, and because language has been conceptualised the world over as a part of culture that can be learned by members of different cultures" (Mead cited in Birdwhistell, 1970, p. 108). If systems do not work in synchrony, then there is a risk that they will act antagonistically in the learning process. From a learning perspective, two conclusions can be drawn from this.

a. Non "language" systems can act as good entry points to the learning of "language".

b. The learning experience needs to be complexified rather than simplified. This means that natural language in action should not be presented, in the first instance, stripped from its links with other systems. Learning needs to begin with authentic language in authentic contexts and then be subjected to a process of investigation by the learner through the use of appropriate tools and feedback mechanisms. Some of these processes may include but will not be limited to simplification or explanation or supported observation of language acts in different contexts. All of these will help to enhance the potential by learners to make sense of what they are observing. These remarks argue strongly for the use of authentic materials in language learning at every stage of the process provided an appropriate environment and support structures are set in place.

g. Following the above arguments, it becomes clear that what language-teachers are teaching and what language learners believe are learning is not (only) the thing that linguists call "language". There are many other things that are learned and taught in high proficiency language learning but not always categorized or understood. Learners often need to know, and often work with, the unknown, the invisible, the uncategorized, the unpredicted and the unpredictable. Learning systems need to be constructed in such a way that these unknowns can be taken account of and incorporated in the learning process albeit they remain unknown/invisible.

h. Humans are physiological beings with limits imposed on them by their bodies though great plasticity also exists.

To summarise the main points so far: "Our objective is to create facilities which make it possible for different perspectives to collide and for the participants to explore forms of legitimation in terms of which they construct and enact reality". (Lian, A. B., 2003). To be consistent with this statement, (language) learning systems need to create opportunities for collisions between individuals' internal systems of understanding and rich language activities. Consequence of this are:

a. Learners' needs, predicted, unpredicted (and unpredictable) will be made visible. These needs result from the attempts of individuals (and their individual histories) to cope with the tasks at hand.

b. Because needs are unpredicted, unpredictable, involving infinite combinations of mutually reinforcing modalities and thus very likely to be different from one learner to the other, it is not logically possible to offer a sequenced (or externally scaffolded) intervention strategy capable of simultaneously meeting the needs of all. Entry points to solving individual problems are likely to be different from person to person. This means that the notion of a tree-like structure for determining a learner's path through a learning system is not optimal. A more interesting approach would be to try and create a learning system based on the notion of the rhizome i.e. a set of conditions which allows for multiple, non-hierarchical entry and exit points in data representation and interpretation (Deleuze & Guattari, 1987, pp. 6-7). This is the very antithesis of a tree structure. A rhizomatic structure can be thought of as a structure which contains components where each and every component is connected to each and every other component of the (living and potentially infinite) structure. In a learning structure it means that learners are able to connect from any activity or information point to any other activity or information point according to perceived need. A rhizomatic structure should not be thought of as chaotic but rather as a self-regulating structure responsive to the learners' needs as determined by the mechanisms in place (human or otherwise) for determining such needs. The rhizome is a critical feature of the language learning system to be described.

The essentially postmodern views that underpin the statements made above cohere well with the following summary of the intellectual position adopted in this paper: "Postmodernist insights require a major shift in our conception of inquiry. No longer should we see ourselves as seeking to uncover a pre-existing reality; rather, we are involved in an interactive process of knowledge *creation*.

We are developing a "working understanding of reality and life, one which suits our purposes" (Beck, 1993, Inquiry section, para 1).

Activity space

The above discussion has identified the general characteristics of desirable language learning environments. The next section will sketch out some environments which have been developed within the above framework and which have shown success.

All the environments share the following characteristics:

a. They create spaces for collisions to occur between learners' logical and representational systems by requiring them to engage in complex real-life (or at least realistic) tasks with genuine communicative stakes.

b. These tasks necessarily require learners to access, understand and possibly reproduce or replicate, parody or otherwise demonstrate an understanding of observed language events. In so doing, they will be exposed to a broad range of problems which they will need to solve in order to make the necessary progress and complete the tasks.

c. The nature of the environments is such that learners of most, if not all, proficiency levels are able to learn personally relevant information and processes and make appropriate contributions.

d. All environments have support structures available to guide learners through individual problems and needs as required. At the most rudimentary level, this support will take the shape of an "all-knowing" teacher or adviser. In more developed systems, there will be contact with the relevant linguistic community as well as audiovisual and software support. The more developed the system the more problems can be solved simultaneously for the group as a whole and the more efficient and effective the system.

Experiments have been conducted in recent and not so recent times within this framework. All have shown good results but all have also suffered from a lack of sufficient resources for self-managed work. Two environments will be summarised below. Others can be found in Ania Lian et al. (2004).

The first environment to be described involved students of French at the University of Queensland, Brisbane, Australia, in a macrosimulation revolving around the creation of a French village (Mestre & Lian, 1985). This was a long-term simulation where participants were required literally to create a village in France, build houses and other buildings, generate local institutions and ways of life. They were required to select personae, to determine their characters and to act out their roles for a whole semester. After a while, they developed a sense of their own history in the simulation and their personal stakes changed: they were no longer just doing an exercise, their "self" was at risk. Their activities were videotaped and time was set aside for observations and analysis of their performances by teachers and other students. Support was available from the teachers in the program and a few native speakers. Available resources included a small selection of books, dictionaries, videocassettes and audiotapes. Resources available nowadays, some twenty years later, can significantly enrich the learning experience.

The second environment involved a group of Master and Doctoral level students in TESOL and foreign language teaching at the University of Canberra, Australia. Their task was to create a radio program for the local community radio station. In order to achieve this and to do so on schedule, they had to wrestle with the realities of a radio station, to understand how radio programs work on community radio, to learn the various discursive genres associated with the undertaking and to act out the roles which they had selected in ways which were acceptable to the local community. Feedback from the community indicated that they achieved significant success despite limited resources and difficulty in accessing them. Like the French students, though, they did develop a sense of their own history within their task.

These environments all provide spaces where collisions can occur between learners' logical and representational systems and the world. While standard textbook and exercise-driven teaching structures may be able to do some of that to a limited extent, they are unlikely to provide a level of complexity sufficient to enable learners to "confront, contrast and contest their understandings and beliefs against the complexity of events which are unfolding around them". In other words, exercise-driven approaches are too "low-level" though they are useful in some of the focused activities which are required from time to time.

Software tools

While the learning spaces referred to above were successful, they all suffered from a lack of resources capable of meeting the individual needs of learners as and when they were required. The tools now to be described represent an attempt to deal with that problem. While these tools all fit within the intellectual structure described earlier and are motivated by it, they can be incorporated into more traditional contexts and will continue to provide the benefits which they were designed to produce.

General characteristics

The tools all share the following general features:

a. From a technical perspective, they are all part of an open-ended set of local and distributed computer programs and other support systems. While the tools are modular for maximum flexibility, portability and individual use, they are all related to one another and can all connect to one another. Connectivity provides additional functionality as opposed to the stand-alone versions.

b. They all have a strong focus on increasing understanding, awareness-raising and critical analytical thinking by giving learners the opportunity to test out their various hypotheses. All tools provide learners with opportunities to confront, contrast and contest their understandings against observed language phenomena through the feedback provided.

c. They all provide on-demand access to information.

d. They all provide a way of questioning the system and the data by making selections, by clicking on words/phrases or on a button. In some cases, the information requested may be tailored to respond to the learners' perceived needs. In other instances, the learners themselves can generate specific lessons on specific points of interest.

e. They all place learners in control of their activities and encourage learner autonomy.

f. They all incorporate the ability to allow learners not only to retrieve but to produce language in one form or another and to help them develop self-awareness.

g. Where appropriate, many of the programs contain automatic feedback systems such as answer markup procedures (to identify incorrect parts of learners' written answers) and/or awareness and self-awareness tools such as visual displays of intonation and automatic low-pass filtering of students' answers to facilitate auditory comparisons between the "native-speaker" production and the learners' productions. They also incorporate enhanced standard language laboratory comparison functions.

h. All programs incorporate load-reduction mechanisms to the extent that it is possible/desirable and, in some cases, *over*loading mechanisms to enable students to practice processing language under greater pressure than would otherwise be the case.

i. Most importantly, they are all able to connect to Web-based database management systems. This provides a high level of "at-will" connectivity between the programs, teaching resources, communication and the general Internet if necessary. These databases are at the heart of the system and enables pointers to be set to appropriate resources, exercises, analysis and self-analysis tools and other systems. The databases enable the system to function rhizomatically. There are no fixed entry or exit points. Learners access the system according to the demands which they happen to be facing at any particular time. For instance, they may want to develop their listening skills. In that case, they may choose to access a listening comprehension program. On the other hand they may want some information about laws relating to the renting of an apartment in Paris. They could question the databases for information and would then be pointed to appropriate resources. Where they move onto next is totally open to conjecture and would depend on a number of unknown/unknowable factors.

By observing interactions, asking questions, generating custom-made exercises, obtaining automatic feedback, processing text under reduced or increased load conditions, developing self-awareness and linking across many sources of information all at a time and place of their choosing, means that the likelihood of learners' needs being met is higher than would otherwise be the case. While this is true in today's mass market of language learning, it is also true in a 1-teacher:1-learner model (often intuitively touted as the ideal). The truth is that no single teacher can possibly know everything that there is to know nor could that teacher provide instantaneous access to the myriad of authentic multimedia documents required, let alone the load-lightening and feedback procedures available only through electronic means. Significantly too, these systems also necessarily promote autonomy as the learners go about their tasks, thus enhancing their research skills and their ability to learn how to learn.

The database

Web-based databases of multimedia documents are at the centre of the learning environment. The taxonomy used to organise the data was developed some years ago by Lian, A. B. (1996) in the context of the *MMBase* database (Lian & Lian, 1994) and was subsequently augmented to reflect growing interest in relating gesture to speech. Examples of categories include functions, notions, grammar, contexts and power relationships between interlocutors. The categories also include intonation classifiers and gestural classifiers. Very importantly, the database provides links and pointers within each document to the micro and macro contexts of the language activity of interest. The system can also provide links to a multitude of other documents—which may reside at remote locations (perhaps in another part of the world).

Learners can interrogate the database directly or it can be accessed by other programs. This combination of features provides the infrastructure for a properly rhizomatic learning structure, offering a very large number of possible entry and exit points.

As an example, let us imagine that a learner wishes to inquire about the workings of "yes-no" questions in French. The learner queries the system according to criteria he/she has selected (e.g. a yes-no question within the context of a greeting) and has a list of instances of yes-no questions returned. The learner examines instances of interest by viewing (and of course listening to) extracts from multimedia documents (perhaps a series of movies) which are relevant. They observe the contexts of language use and reflect on the ways these yes-no questions operate. They then identify and compare further instances of such questions drawn from the same movie as, for reasons best known to themselves, they have now decided to compare the ways in which a specific movie treats these questions. They then decide to expand their search beyond the context of greetings. Their curiosity triggered by what they have seen and heard, they decide to view the entire movie from which the questions are extracted. As they view the movie, they stop to check their comprehension of the particular events unfolding before them and, at the same time, sharpen their understandings of communication in French. After these enriching experiences, they return to their original point of departure and ask the computer system to generate a series of focused lessons for which they themselves have set the parameters. Finally, they return to whatever original task had triggered their interest in the first place.

The above example clearly illustrates the rhizomatic nature of the experience. An arbitrary (relevant to the learner) entry point was selected. It happened to be a grammatical structure but it could have been a function (e.g. a greeting) or a genre (e.g. an advertisement), a gesture or a facial expression (e.g. raised eyebrows). The learner then went on a serendipitous adventure which was supported at every step of the way by lessons and other forms of learning infrastructure capable of establishing a form of dialogic inquiry between learner and text. The path selected was in no way predetermined and was made possible only because of the connectivity provided by the database system and, of course, the speed of retrieval.

At every step of the way, plentiful opportunity was provided for collisions to occur between what learners knew (their personal histories/perceptions/internal logical and representational systems) and what they were encountering as the support systems were constructed to facilitate such collisions (for some examples see below). In their data-surfing, learners would have encountered and dealt with not only what they expected to find or, indeed, what the support systems had identified as valuable, but also unpredicted and unpredictable instances of communicative phenomena at work which the very act of comparing across contexts would have brought to their attention and possibly clarified for them at a personal level.

The description of activities just provided is not fanciful. All programs referred to have already been developed in proof-of-concept mode over the space of several years and now need to be integrated. That integration has already begun as will be illustrated by brief overviews of three programs: *MMExplore*, *Dialgen* and *MMGen*.

MMExplore

MMExplore (Lian, Lian & Puakpong, 2003) is a refinement of its predecessor *MMBrowse* (Lian & Lian, 1995). It is a system designed to enable the exploration of authentic text in a variety of ways with special emphasis on the development of listening skills. It enables learners to discover, observe and reflect on the meanings of individual texts while varying the processing load.

In order to achieve this, the program offers learners a written transcript of the passage where each letter in every word has been replaced with an asterisk (*). The learners' task is to discover the words underneath the asterisks and recreate the text. In so doing, they will gain an understanding of the passage, come to grips with the features of the text and engage in many discoveries and develop self-awareness along the way.

Load-lightening is built into all aspects of the program's operation. For instance, learners have the ability to view or listen to any arbitrarily-selected portion of text in a variety of modes: full audiovisual, audio only or video only (with further modifications as indicated below). In support of their "raw" viewing/listening they are given further help through the "starred" transcript and other inferencing and guessing exercises, explanations and glosses. These explanations and glosses are available automatically in response to learners' interactions with the system but they can also be provided on demand. Learners click on words or chunks of language in a variety of ways and receive different forms of feedback either from the program itself or from a remote database.

Further load-lightening of "raw" multimedia information is provided through electronic low-pass digital filtering of speech to highlight intonation patterns, as well as forward and backward build-up of speech in order to bring out previously undetected features of the spoken language. Underloading and overloading is provided through the use of distortion-free electronically slowed-down, accelerated or "noisy" language. Built into the system is a sophisticated answer-evaluation system (based on Lian, 1984) which, by virtue of the nature of its feedback is able to help learners to modify their perceptions and develop new understandings of how communication works. It also enables learners to record their voice and compare it immediately with that of the text being studied thus providing enhanced language laboratory functionality with the added advantage of being able to use any authentic text selected for inclusion in the system.

Additional functionality is to be provided through the inclusion of visual support through the display of intonation curves for both the native-speaker model and the learner's own productions. The ability to enhance learners' judgements in relation to their own pronunciation will be provided in due course through the addition of real-time low-pass filtering for learner productions.

Not all functions are made available at all times as the system adopts a problem-solving approach where learners need first to grapple with difficulties rather than be provided with the relief of "the correct answer". Finally, *MMExplore* lends itself to a multitude of activities, including the analysis of gesture. Crucially though, *MMExplore* is only one of the open-ended set of modules which can be linked to the database which, in turn, provides both the information displayed to learners and the ability to connect to other sources of information.

Together, these support structures will ultimately lead not only to an awareness of communication at work but also to the development of enhanced self-awareness. Further, users of this program are catering to their own needs, motivations or preferences in ways which would simply be impossible in a regimented/text-controlled lock-stepped environment.

It is worth remembering though that while the program is useful of itself, its value increases considerably because of its connectivity features.

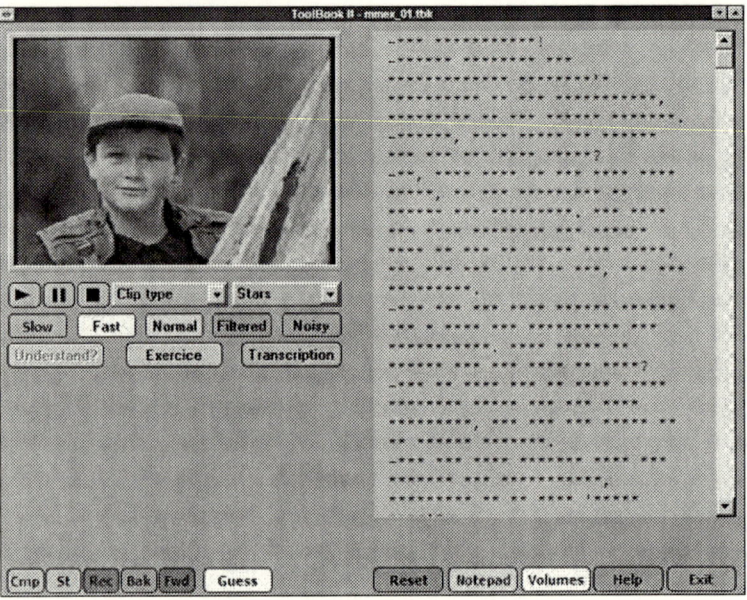

Figure 1 MMExplore screen layout

The descriptions of other programs which now follow are much briefer as they all contain more or less the same kinds of features described above. Descriptions will now focus on differences between programs. Further, the screen displays will be more or less self-explanatory if the general features described in this paper are kept in mind.

Dialgen: A dialogue generator and dialogue practice system

Dialgen is a system designed to provide opportunities for speaking practice (Lian & Joy, 1983; Lian, 1994). It consists of a program which generates authentic-like dialogues which learners can then listen to in part or in whole. They can observe and question on a word-by-word, chunk-by-chunk or sentence-by-sentence basis. Perceptual support is provided by way of low-pass filtering as well as language-laboratory functionality. A self-awareness feature enables learners to record their voices and to listen to themselves as if they were one of the participants in the dialogue being studied. A simulation mode provides a timing constraint that learners need to adapt to. In this mode, learners "participate" in the conversation by adopting a role and by being given turns by the program during which they should speak. Each turn is timed and learners have to learn to comply with the rhythms of natural conversations. This is a way of letting the rhythms of speech write themselves on learners in a way which is psychologically safe but also enforces the demands of real life. While, in the first instance, this will almost certainly overload learners, it provides a worthwhile and interesting challenge and learners have been observed to adapt well to the procedure. Again, this program has links to a central database and can either act as a starting point in the rhizomatic sequence or as one of the many possible stops along the learning sequence.

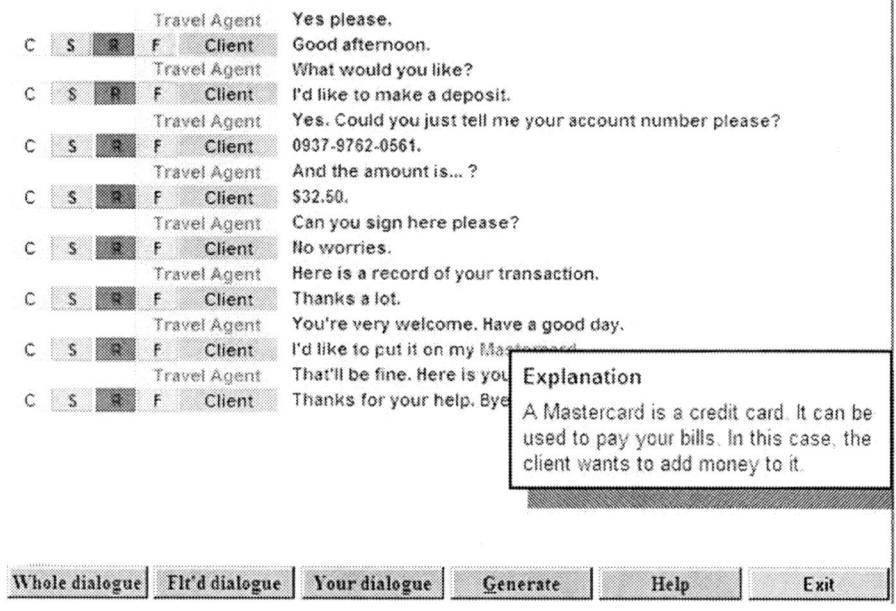

Figure 2 Dialgen screen layout

MMGen: A lesson generator

An interesting possibility which a database-managed approach offers is that of learners themselves generating their own lessons. This is what *MMGen* helps to achieve. In the example below, learners are investigating how questions work in French. The display shows questions extracted from a French television game show. Where this program differs from other programs described is that before reaching the stage of actually doing the exercises, learners go through a process of selection of the patterns that they wish to study by interrogating the intonation database, examining the descriptions and characteristics of each intonation pattern and then requesting the system to generate the lesson from a series of built-in templates. The result is shown below. The program maintains its connectivity to the database so as to provide additional information and navigation capabilities. Again, close examination of the screen display below will reveal some of the features of the program not discussed here in detail.

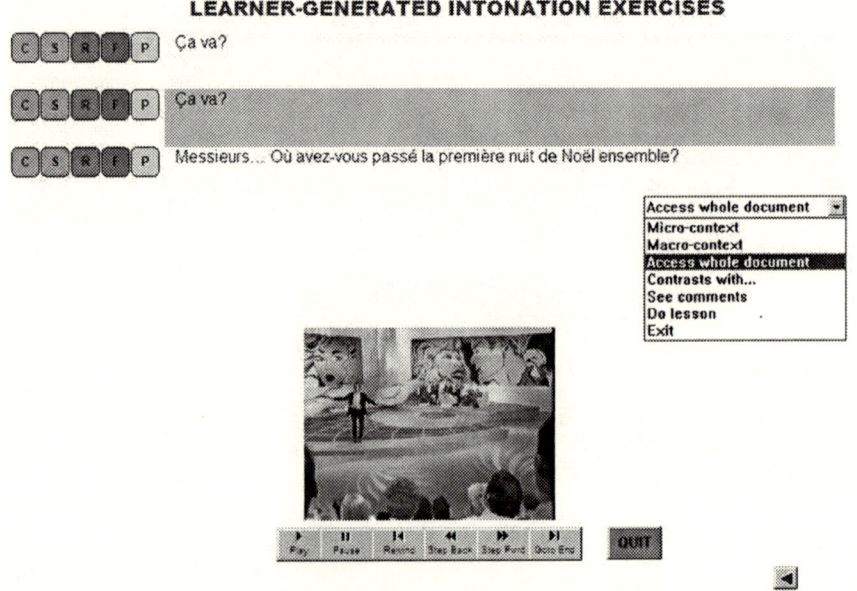

Figure 3 MMGen screen layout

The list of programs described above is by no means complete, nor can the list ever be closed off. Systems like these are fundamentally open-ended and limited only by the technology available at any particular time and, of course, our imagination. As connectivity increases as a result of better and faster networks, the ability to add extra modules with relatively little effort will enable the system to grow in functionality.

Conclusion

Systems like the one described in this paper provide a level of learner support which will become increasingly necessary in a rapidly globalising world where the future of language teaching and learning is in a mass market rather than an elite market. Language learning is likely to be the biggest educational business ever as all citizens will need to know a language other than their own. This is particularly important for the learning of English which is clearly sweeping the world. Many continue striving to achieve some level of communicative proficiency in English. In that context, the language teaching profession and the learning systems which it develops will need to be able to deal with the demands of these new conditions while still remaining true to the requirements of properly conceptualised and responsive teaching and learning approaches.

This chapter has sought to respond to some of the above concerns by introducing an intellectual framework for language teaching based on a postmodern view of the act of learning. This framework then provided the basis for a principled approach to the development of learning environments. A description of such environments was then offered and suggestions were made as to how appropriate individualised technology-enhanced support could be provided.

References

Beck, C. (1993). Postmodernism, pedagogy, and philosophy of education. Retrieved December 2, 2003, from http://www.ed.uiuc.edu/EPS/PES-Yearbook/93_docs/BECK.HTM

Birdwhistell, R. (1971). *Kinesics and context*. Philadelphia: University of Pennsylvania Press.

Bourdieu, P. (1995). *The logic of practice*. Palo Alto: Stanford University Press.

Bourdieu, P. (1991). Language and symbolic power. (Translated by J. B. Thompson), Cambridge, MA: Harvard University Press.

Calhoun, C. (2000). Information technology and the international public sphere. Paper presented to the International Sociological Association, Brisbane, Australia. Retrieved December 2, 2003, from http://www.ssrc.org/programs/calhoun/publications/infotechandpublicsphere.pdf

Deleuze, G. & Guattari, F. (Translation: B. Massumi) (1987). *A thousand plateaus: Capitalism and schizophrenia*. Minneapolis: University of Minnesota Press.

Derrida, J. (1982). Différance. In Derrida, J. (Ed.), *Margins of philosophy* (pp. 1-27). Chicago: The University of Chicago Press.

Freadman, A. (1994). Models of genre for language teaching. Paper delivered as The Sonia Marks Memorial Lecture. Sydney: University of Sydney.

Guberina, P. (1976). Structuration et dépassement des structures perceptives et psycholinguistiques dans la méthodologie SGAV. In *Actes du 3e Colloque international SGAV pour l'enseignement des langues* (pp. 41-58). Paris: Didier.

Guberina, P. (1972). *Restricted bands of frequencies in auditory rehabilitation of deaf*. Zagreb: Institute of Phonetics Faculty of Arts.

Herrmann, C.S. (2003). The Brain generates its own sentence melody: A Gestalt phenomenon in speech perception. In *Brain and Language, 85*(3), 396-401.

Lian, A.B. (1996). The management and distribution of language learning resources in the digital era. Paper presented to the National Conference of the Australian Federation of Modern Language Teachers' Association, Perth, October 1994. In Scarino, A. (Ed.). *Equity in Languages Other Than English* (pp. 177-182). Perth.

Lian, A.B., Dolan, D., Scotellaro, G., & Lian, A.-P. (2004). Narizoma: Critical pedagogy in practice. In this volume.

Lian, A.B. (2003). Beyond illusions and facts: Toward a methodology of dialogue and dialogue-enhancing environments. Paper presented at The International Conference on Computers and Philosophy, ANU, Australia and Rice University, Texas, USA. Retrieved December 2, 2003, from http://www.anialian.com/On_Time.html

Lian, A-P. & Joy, B.K. (1983). The butcher, the baker, the candlestick maker: Some uses of dialogue generators in computer-assisted foreign language learning. In *Australian Review of Applied Linguistics, 6*(2), 60-71.

Lian, A-P. (1984). Aspects of answer-evaluation in traditional computer-assisted language learning. In Russell R. M. (Ed.): *Proceedings of the 2nd CALITE Congress,* pp. 150-160. Brisbane: University of Queensland.

Lian, A-P. (1987). Awareness, autonomy and achievement in foreign language learning. In *Revue de Phonétique Appliquée, 82-84,* 167-184 and available at http://www.andrewlian.com/andrewlian/prowww/Aaa.htm

Lian, A-P. (1990). *IBMREG*: An adaptation for IBM PC of the *MINISCAN* lesson driver (UNIX version), Gold Coast: Bond University Language Centre.

Lian, A-P. (1994). Dialogue generators Mark II. Paper presented to the National Congress of the Applied Linguistics Association of Australia, Melbourne: University of Melbourne.

Lian, A-P. & Lian, A.B. (1995). *MMBrowse: Audiovisual browsing system.* Critical Pedagogy and Technology Consultants Pty Ltd.

Lian, A-P. & Lian, A.B. (1997). The secret of the Shao-Lin monk: Contribution to an intellectual framework for language learning. In *On-CALL,* May, 2-19. Brisbane: Centre for Language Teaching and Research, University of Queensland, and available at http://www.andrewlian.com/andrewlian/prowww/shaolin/psupres2.htm

Lian, A-P. (2000). From first principles: Constructing language learning and teaching environments. Keynote address to the 9th International Symposium and Bookfair, English Teachers' Association of the Republic of China, Taipei. In *Selected Papers from the Ninth International Symposium on English Teaching,* 49-62. Taipei: Crane Publishing. Available at http://www.andrewlian.com/andrewlian/prowww/first_principles/index.html

Lian, A-P. (2001). Imagination in language teaching and learning. Keynote address to the English Language Teaching and Knowledge Transformation Conference, Chaoyang University of Technology, Taichung, Taiwan. In *Proceedings* of the Conference and available at http://www.andrewlian.com/andrewlian/prowww/imagination/index.html

Lian, A-P. & Lian, A.B. (2002). *MMBase.* An audiovisual database. Critical Pedagogy and Technology Consultants Pty Ltd.

Lian, A-P. & Lian, A.B. (2003). *Dialgen*. A prototype dialogue practice system for second language learning. Critical Pedagogy and Technology Consultants Pty Ltd.

Lian, A-P. & Lian, A. B. & Puakpong, N. (2003). MMExplore. An audiovisual listening comprehension development program. Critical Pedagogy and Technology Consultants Pty Ltd.

Mestre, M-C. & Lian, A-P. (1985). Goal-directed communicative interaction and macrosimulation. In *Revue de Phonétique Appliquée, 73-75*, 185-210. Paris: Didier, and available at http://www.andrewlian.com/andrewlian/prowww/macrosim.htm

Minsky, M. (1981). Music, mind, and meaning. *Computer Music Journal, 5*(3). Retrieved December 2, 2003, from http://web.media.mit.edu/~minsky/papers/MusicMindMeaning.html

Renard, R. (1978). *Introduction à la méthode verbo-tonale*. Paris: Didier.

2

Narizoma: Critical pedagogy in practice

Ania Lian, Debbie Dolan, Grazia Scotellaro and Andrew Lian

Abstract

This chapter discusses the concept of Narizoma: a web-based educational environment currently under development. The discussion focuses on the collaborative aspects of the environment and therefore on the kinds of pedagogic demands that teaching institutions as a whole, rather than single departments or individual teachers, may need to respond to, if they wish to help support such a complex community at work. Characteristics of Narizoma are that it is a large and complex environment. It is ongoing (potentially forever), engaging students in an increasingly complex web of issues which then feeds back into their daily lives. It is autopoietic because the lives of the participants constantly generate new issues. These issues develop as a result of need rather than from pre-determined content. Its objectives and structure emerge from ongoing discussions in the literature in relation to the quality of communication that information technology systems can make available to us and the potential that enhancing these qualities may contribute to education in general, and second language learning in particular. The discussion which leads to the description of the Narizoma environment brings to focus on the issue of the intellectual framework which would provide a basis for creating such negotiating structures. The concept of the Narizoma environment is presented against the background of a number of educational projects conducted by the authors over the years. All these environments share the principles of Narizoma and illustrate the contributions that reflective and exploratory learning models can offer.

Introduction

The concept of communication as involving negotiation of the references which are familiar in order to effect a change in the dynamics between people is not without consequences to L2-teaching research and practice. The concept suggests that communication as negotiation leads to generating new forms of reference. This then implies that to learn to communicate does not mean learning a language as such. Rather, it means learning the skills of negotiating i.e. "rules of use without which the rules of syntax are useless" (Hymes, 1996, p. 33).

The understanding that language is both, a means (or terms) for negotiating meaning and, as suggested above, also as a product of this negotiation suggests a very dynamic view of language. It also helps us form a framework which coherently links the concepts of communication and language. But it is a very risky framework. It implies that the logics upon which we build our negotiations are an object of and subject to negotiation. There seems to be nothing stable about language that we could teach the pieces which comprise it, or that make up the knowledge of language. Communication, as a concept which involves negotiation, removes from language teachers the object of their expertise: the language.

This dynamic view of language also shifts the focus of L2-teaching and research away from the issue of 'What to teach and how?'. If communication is always about negotiation, be it between speakers of the same or different languages, then it is impossible to identify the correct protocols or logics which would guarantee that understanding happens. In short, there is nothing that can be taught as such. Furthermore, teaching abstract concepts, in fact, runs contrary to the understanding that communication means negotiation. Thus studies which hope to match learning objectives with specific models of learners (low level, high level, students from different backgrounds, etc.) run the risk that, effectively, they create learning conditions that respond to the learning needs of the constructs of learners that they create, rather than to students' negotiation problems as they experience them.

This risk is reflected in the critique that theories can often suggest the existence of the very problems they are supposedly designed to solve. Thus, in our view, the objective of the learning environment therefore is not to teach, nor is it to leave learners without support. Rather, the focus on negotiation orients L2-teaching research and practice toward identifying the means which would help learners to *break* the logics, or the protocols, that obstruct this negotiation process. The objective therefore is no longer how to teach 'correct logics', but how to ensure that negotiations would not stop. Without negotiation, learning stops, and, therefore, so does communication.

In congruence with this view of L2-teaching research and practice, this chapter describes the concept of Narizoma: a web-based educational environment currently under development. Narizoma means 'New Rhizome'. *Na* is a play on the Greek word for *new/s* and *rizoma* stands for *rhizome* in Italian. Narizoma is being created with the intention of increasing communication opportunities between individuals and groups in spite of whatever differences may exist between them. The idea is to construct an environment which, in order to function in an inclusive way, must come to terms with a number of issues, least of them linguistic differences between its citizens.

In this regard, the hope behind Narizoma is to create conditions where the support which teachers offer, or the citizens of Narizoma themselves, is directed toward overcoming the specific difficulties which living in Narizoma generates. In this way, the pedagogic practices of classrooms, would be geared toward assisting students in the actual communicative interactions which they need to resolve to participate in the life of Narizoma. Of course, this focus does not ensure that the applied forms of assistance will be successful. But it does challenge L2-teaching research and practice to respond to the demands that living in Narizoma places on their students, and, also, it takes pedagogic practices of classrooms outside of the walls of classroom, and therefore outside of the world of abstract knowledge taught to realise abstract objectives.

It may also be the case, that in order to function in Narizoma, students will learn more than one language simultaneously. As said earlier, in Narizoma, the goal is to communicate in order to live, rather than to study a language as such. The main objective behind the structure of Narizoma therefore is to reflect how educational institutions can adapt their intellectual capital to the demands of a truly collaborative structure. The argument of this chapter is that in order to so, it would be necessary to step way from strategies which reinforce divisions between individuals in terms of arbitrarily selected commonalities (linguistic or disciplinary) and instead, to focus on ways in which the *quality* of students' interactions could be enhanced and assisted.

The discussion which leads to the description of Narizoma focuses on this aspect of the environment. It does so by foregrounding the concept of dialogic learning conceived as directed toward facilitating forms of interaction which help individuals grow the frames of reference in relation to which they evaluate and hence restructure their communicative behaviour.

The concept of dialogic learning and CALL-based environments

The concept of *dialogic learning* as used in this chapter is different from that generally applied in the sociocultural approaches in SLA (cf. Lantolf, 2000). *Dialogue* here does not describe a process of progressive build up toward mastery (Lantolf, 2000, pp. 17-18). Rather, it involves individuals in critiquing or revising the terms in relation to which their interactions are played out (cf. Latour, 2000). Thus the two concepts of dialogue are very different. In Lantolf, the dialogue serves to 'recreate history' by creating experts in the process where individuals first "move through stages" until "finally they gain control over their own social and cognitive activities" (Lantolf, 2000, p. 17). Here, on the other hand, dialogue serves for 'escaping history' i.e. "generating more ideas than we have received" (Latour, 2002). It is a process which involves a *collision* of perspectives whose sources of validation and capacity to enhance understandings take the form of an object of investigation, not acquisition.

A dialogue of this kind does not aim at recreating experts as it does not construct a person into a specific position. Rather, the objective is to involve individuals in reflecting upon or testing the concepts in terms of which they act in order to identify their explanatory power in relation to other rival perspectives. In this sense, dialogue is not conceptualised as structures which *reproduce* history, but which effect change. Dialogue therefore is seen as contexts where *histories collide* and where negotiation occurs between contrasting or incommensurable positions. An outcome of this process of collision and negotiation are more informed perspectives i.e. perspectives which are more aware of own limitations and, as such, more critical. We can thus conclude that dialogue, as conceptualised in here, involves a change in the dynamics between concepts that inform our actions, effectively expanding these concepts and, and, as a result, effecting change.

Most importantly, though, it would seem that this change in the dynamics will depend on the extent to which the negotiations help to bring in new elements powerful enough to reveal tension between elements or perspectives which otherwise appear commensurable while, in fact, obstructing expansion and learning. In the context of L2-teaching, the difficulty in achieving this goal is compounded in models which conflate language with culture and which suggest that groups which are separated by language are also separated by culture. It is our argument that an assumption of this kind immediately removes any platform for dialogue and learning. It leaves individuals nothing to negotiate and build upon as it creates an unassailable gap between linguistically different groups. With no frames of reference available for students to compare, contrast and, in the process, restructure, the teaching models offer no framework which would explain how the learning is to take place. L1 and L2 speakers are conceptualised as belonging to two different worlds, each for itself, and each developing in isolation from the other. This is the case, for instance, in recent studies conducted by Kramsch & Thorne (2002) and Furstenberg, Levet, English & Maillet (2001).

Both projects involve CMC-based interactions between American and French students. Both projects adopt a methodology where the object of investigation is the *other* culture and the *other* language. Both involve students discussing these although neither study proposes frames of reference which the discussions are to follow. Consequently, as Kramsch and Thorne's (2002) study shows, it was *not* the frames of reference that were on trial but the students themselves. Furthermore, as Eric's (an American student) commentary shows, for the entire duration of the study neither group quite understood what the interactions were meant to achieve: "[I]t seems true that they weren't doing the same thing we were. It seemed like, you know, we had a task. And they, it seemed like, I didn't know what they were doing" (Thorne, 2003, p. 45).

To explain this confusion, Thorne uncritically adopts the argument of the 'cultural divide': "Trust and relationship-building for the Americans and truth value and negotiation of factual accuracy for the French involved differing goals, frames of reference, and perceptions of what is desirable, and even possible, though Internet-based communicative activity" (Thorne, 2003, p. 46). He does so without attempting to consider that the divide did not emerge naturally but was imposed by the very framework of the course and effectively prevented students from questioning its meaning and, in the process, building upon shared frames of reference. It is the divide implied in the methodology of the course that made Eric speak about "us and the French" (Thorne, 2003, p. 45).

As in the Kramsch and Thorne study, interactions in the *Cultura* project are also directed toward creating a *picture of the other* thus reinforcing, rather than seeking to overcome, the unassailable gap which engaging in this activity creates between the foreign and target language speakers. The project leaders thus speak about "developing students' understanding of another culture" (Furstenberg et al, 2001, p. 57), enabling them "to look at the universe through the eyes of others" (Furstenberg et al, 2001, p. 58), and the project offering "both sets of students" (Furstenberg et al, 2001, p. 59), the French and the Americans, "on both sides of the Atlantic a unique comparative, cross-cultural approach for gradually constructing knowledge of other values, attitudes, and beliefs, in ever-widening approach to understanding the foreign culture" (Furstenberg et al, 2001, p. 57).

As the project asserts, "Explicating these differences is one way to develop cultural literacy" (Furstenberg et al, 2001, p. 75). However, since the explications were to be constructed within the language-specific cultures it seems plausible to argue that they would be framed *monologically* and not *dialogically* thus lacking a platform which would allow students to identify the explanatory power of the differences that they identified. This is why discussions about culture do not necessarily generate understandings of culture:

> Given that, even for native speakers within French educational systems the explicit teaching of canonical culture regularly fails to produce legitimate cultural ease, how much less likely is it that foreign-language classrooms will provide their students with functional skills for that kind of performance? (Cryle, 1996, p. 281).

The tendency to see language as unifying its users in a single frame of reference (culture) is widely spread in L2-teaching research. It is our view that learning activities which link A language with A culture do not only propagate the belief in *one's own culture* on the one hand, and *the culture of others* on the other (Chambers, 1996, p. 144), they also provide no conceptual basis for constructing a platform for intercultural dialogue and hence are counterproductive in relation to the very goals which they hope to realise (de Nooy, 1996; Freadman, 1994). However if, as Thorne mentions, culture mediates *human activities* (Thorne, 2003, p. 40), culture can be seen as tied to the frames of reference (i.e., the interplay of various forms of value, or capital, cf. Bourdieu, 1991) in terms of which these activities are constructed.

Furthermore, since it is impossible to trace the historical developments of the American and the French people (or indeed any other people) to the point where it is possible to claim that a complete separation of the cultural frames of reference has occurred, it would seem that whatever understandings individuals form, they do so in the context of practices and in relation to those practices. It would follow that the objective of (cultural) learning cannot be to understand the *other* (and in the process to create the *other*), but to 'work' with the other. In other words, the aim is not to see the "other" as located in language, but in the various forms of reference which are sourced in practices and which, therefore, are irreducible to language. In this way, the "other" does not divide, but functions as building blocks which help everyone, irrespectively of their language, test the assumptions about practices with which they enter their communicative contexts.

In this model, practices, or forms of engagement, provide a space necessary for a dialogue of this kind to emerge and for learning to happen.

The idea of engaging students in contexts which challenge their established frames of reference and, in the process, help them expand these, is congruent with the concerns expressed by Calhoun (Calhoun, 2002) regarding Information Technology. He sees it as a priority to resolve the problem of the effectiveness of communicative spaces.

A short description of the TNN (Thai News Network) project is presented below as an example of a way in which technology could play such a supportive function. The TNN project was a pilot study conducted in Thailand, with first year undergraduate students of Thai, with the objective of facilitating the sort of reflective environment discussed above (Buranapatana & Lian, 2002). The TNN project also functioned as a precursor to the Narizoma project.

TNN (Thai News Network)—the precursor to Narizoma

The idea of creating a Thai News Network information channel was born out of projects and university courses which engaged students in a number of macro-activities. Some of those took place at the University of Queensland's Department of French and engaged students in the contexts of practices of specific target communities. Examples of such activities included: *Creating and living in a French village* (Lian & Mestre, 1985), and *Creating a day on French TV*. Another stream of similar projects relates to the projects conducted by Scotellaro from 1997 in partnership with ItalyCa (Italian Radio Program) and Tuttifrutti (youth multicultural radio program). These projects involved students from a number of high schools in Canberra, Australia, producing Italian radio broadcasts for the Community Multicultural Services. Several years on, some of those original students continue to this day to be involved in broadcasting. The success of the projects can be gauged from the fact that there is continuing cooperation between the Community Multicultural Services radio station and the Australian National University whose students of Italian participate regularly in the production of radio programs as part of their standard language-learning activities.

The concept of involving students in the production of radio broadcasts was subsequently translated into a project where students from Khon Kaen University, Thailand, undertook to develop an Internet-based information channel TNN (Thai News Network). The project was part of a course on critical reading in Thai. Although it had no L2-component, it offers some general principles for thinking about the ways in which technology could be of assistance in contexts which challenge learners' ability to *affect* the dynamics of their interactions. On reading the literature (e.g., Freebody, Luke, & Gilbert, 1991), it became apparent that for the environment to offer such challenging conditions, it was important to create structures where students not only engage in the criticism of texts but also, more importantly, do so in order to *enhance* their interactions with others (Buranapatana & Lian 2002). With this objective in mind, the project of the Thai News Network was proposed to students from Khon Kaen University, Thailand, who embraced it both with some fears and great enthusiasm. As the students themselves reported:

> I was interested in taking part in the experiment because we had been informed by the researcher that we would enhance our critical thinking abilities so I wanted to see how I would go.

Another student wrote:

> I have never ever worked so hard before. In the beginning I did not work much because I never had to before, so I did not know how to do it. My teacher explained everything clearly but I did not understand how to start working.

The objectives of the course were based in pedagogies which derive from the concerns of critical theory. Their goal can be summarised as constructing conditions which *enhance* students' informed participation in the contexts of life. It is this goal of *enhancing* informed participation that the project sees as critical to the process of creating a platform toward a form of empowerment that helps individuals and groups "to transform their circumstances for themselves by themselves" (Tripp, 1992, p. 13). Students themselves understood the power of informed participation. A number of them expressed excitement that their work was no longer to be an essay for the teacher to grade but was directed toward creating a resonance in those who would come to their website: "I think presenting our work on the TNN website is an important way to encourage all the students in the experimental group to work harder..." Another student wrote: "When writing on-line articles, I always thought of the readers and what they might say." Comments from the public which included people from within the university and outside were posted on the site as well as the discussions which they generated.

A number of strategies were employed to assist students in the exploration of the contexts, understandings and practices in relation to which they were positioning their own stories. The main aspect of their journey, that about which almost all students reported, revolved around the search for information. Students often reported on learning to use the libraries in a far more interesting and useful manner than before and to search the Internet. Importantly, they also learnt to look for information outside libraries, reading newspapers, searching the Internet, or looking for people who could offer them more insights. Students themselves spoke about this aspect of the project:

> In the beginning of this course, we were not ready to learn in this way. [...] We tried very hard to search for more information from the Internet, journals, magazines, and other sources. We were surprised that we got more information from more sources than we expected.

The most important aspect of this form of exploratory learning was that students were not directed to any specific sources of information. Instead, they were told about choices and shown ways to exercise those choices. There was no pedagogic agenda which would lock them into specific forms interactions. The only elements that united all the explorations was the desire to be understood i.e. validated as coherent and making a contribution. Students' searches for information were backed up with various field trips, talks to other people, other students and villagers. The students met a chemistry professor who gave them time and spoke to them at length on the issue of interest to them (spirulina).

Students also held general meetings of the entire group to stimulate further exchange between them. In this way they obtained useful clues about their thoughts from other students who, at the same time, were working on different issues and reading different things. The diversity of activities that students undertook illustrates the point that the environment was constructed with the objective of enhancing opportunities for dialogue to occur rather than for students to depend on information solely from the computer. This is also a very important aspect of discussions which foreground concerns that some students may not be able to match their peers from privileged backgrounds with equal computer power. Within the context of TNN, not a single student complained about technology because the objectives of the course did not depend on technology. Rather, the aim was to explore opportunities available in order to facilitate dialogue. Technology was only a part of the means toward making this goal possible.

The TNN pilot study provided some interesting insights in relation to Narizoma. Most of all, it showed that dialogic activity, even though supported by on-line resources, needs not be limited to those who are on-line. In fact, the TNN-study showed that a richer and more far-reaching dialogic platform is established when students explored both the on-line and off-line sources. Moreover, the off-line interlocutors need not necessarily be directly involved with students' on-line projects. This way of linking on-line and off-line environments around students is rather different from settings which make on-line exchanges the focus and which, as a result, remove students (and their forms of engagement) from their local communities. The TNN-project sought to protect students from such isolationist tendencies thus helping individuals to construct their various forms of engagement in a manner which does not dislocate them from either of their contexts of participation.

As students' comments reveal, the TNN project enjoyed great success: "" The success of TNN was also shared among the University faculty. All this also illustrates that within the confines of universities and course syllabi, there is plenty of room for experimental projects which, by virtue of being different, help to achieve goals which ordinary classes may miss.

Currently the TNN project is undergoing revision and a number of changes will be implemented in order to make room for forms of expression and action that have not been included so far. The project will seek involvement from students from other classes or universities from Thailand, Australia and elsewhere. However its main goal will remain the same: inspiring creativity on the part of whoever is involved in order to enhance communication between them. This is also the goal of the Narizoma environment which provides a larger framework for projects such as TNN or any other project which may be generated as a result of the possibilities that it offers.

Narizoma

The Narizoma environment has been conceptualised with the aim of enlarging the contexts of interaction for projects such as TNN to allow for a greater intersection of ideas and issues than projects like TNN alone can generate. Narizoma is the name of a virtual (Internet-based) community constructed in such a way as to enable its inhabitants to create a way of life as they would want it to be and in terms that they collectively decide upon. It is a space to be filled with history and hence with everything that life brings. The challenge of Narizoma therefore is relatively simple: it is a potential alternative to the current social structures inasmuch as its shape and the way of life that it takes on do not depend on reality as we have come to know it but on the decisions which will be made within it. Whatever the problems, the citizens of Narizoma should find ways of solving them. The aim is to give participants the possibility to shape their destinies in ways that reflect how they would like Narizoma to be.

The general objectives of the Narizoma environment are no different from those of TNN. The main goal is to enhance the quality of interactions between individuals and/or groups while, at the same time, not removing the link which joins the participants with the world outside the on-line confines of Narizoma. The environment is designed to facilitate such a link and, as a result, it functions as a platform for negotiating the beliefs that come from the contexts other than Narizoma (the "old world") in the contexts of conditions which apply in Narizoma (the "new world") and vice versa. As these interactions grow, it is possible that the ideas from Narizoma may impact upon the ways of the "old world". Movement the other way is also inevitable. Because Narizoma is an open space, it is planned that the only citizens of Narizoma can be students from educational institutions. The greatest advantage that we see in Narizoma is the fact that it sets up *no* other constraints thus allowing for interactions to be driven by intersecting agenda rather than by agenda which would prevent such criss-crossing. Thus, Narizoma helps to bring to the surface the more and the less salient concerns which reflect the historically-shaped experiences of their participants i.e. the different tensions in terms of which they structure their solidarity relationships (national, political, class oriented, linguistic, professional, disciplinary; cf. Calhoun, 2003). It allows for people to meet and communicate who otherwise would not be likely to do so. It allows for investigating issues which have a larger than disciplinary focus.

In this perspective, Narizoma has the potential to respond to the challenge issued by the sociologists who are concerned with the Internet being used mainly to reinforce the already-established connections thus contributing amazingly little to reshaping the current structures which underlie thought and action (cf. DiMaggio et al, 2001). As signaled by Calhoun (2002), to effect such a change would require practical experiments based on an idealistic vision where "rational-critical debate improves the quality of opinions, educates the participants and forms a collective understanding of issues that advances beyond pre-existing definitions of interests or identities" (p. 19).

Moreover, without such models, it may be that our use of information technology will remain reduced to isolated "websites giv[ing] the impression of consisting simply of the spontaneous postings of the public" (Calhoun 2002, p. 15). It is hoped that Narizoma will rectify this status quo while also giving researchers a chance to participate actively in this goal. In this task, researchers are challenged to change their own relationship to information technology and the Internet in particular. To effect change, the Internet need no longer be just a laboratory (DiMaggio et al, 2001, p. 329) but a means for creating spaces which enhance dialogue and, as a result, awareness.

How would Narizoma work?

Like TNN, the Narizoma project is designed as a space for experimental learning projects. As in TNN, the issues that life in Narizoma generates should form the contexts for projects which students, together with the support structures around them (other students, teams of teachers, parents, members of the public who may be consulted, literature, privately-available technological support or support accessed through schools or universities, various browsing tools attached to Narizoma and those developed in due course by its citizens) will undertake. Thus students' engagement in Narizoma can take multiple paths. They can partake in the environment out of curiosity, or as a result of curricular (or extracurricular) activities designed to enhance their interdisciplinary skills, or as an experimental project carried out within the standard curriculum where disciplinary objectives (e.g. the study of law, foreign languages, mathematics, information technology, physics) form the specific focus for structuring their contributions to Narizoma.

Because Narizoma is a different world, it does not require from students to become members of specific communities of practice but, rather, it challenges them to reflect on the relationship between what they do and what they seek to achieve. In Narizoma students have a choice to reflect upon the ways in which their specific discipline foci can contribute to life in Narizoma. Thus, how students word the law of Narizoma, apply the law, work with linguistic differences, apply their understandings of mathematics, how they utilise their study of physics or information technology, all depends on how they see their actions to be of value to the community at large. Students' contributions if conducted within the framework of curricular, and thus assessable, university or school subjects can be evaluated with this objective in mind.

The task of shaping and living in a new world will reveal a number of challenges, not the least of which will be linguistic ones. Since the citizens of Narizoma are united in the goal of making Narizoma a liveable and interesting place, the belief is that life in Narizoma will demand a great deal of cooperation between individuals who may be from different linguistic backgrounds. The linguistic demands will be multiple. They may range from students engaging in activities utilising solely their second languages through to activities which would allow students to narrow down the specific language needs which they experience, to specific forms of support that Narizoma may offer. It needs to be stressed that it is the cooperative or collaborative aspect of life in Narizoma that may allow for diversification of the ways in which students attend to the linguistic demands that participation in the environment brings with it. Since Narizoma is likely to bring together students from various linguistic backgrounds, it will be important that communication and exchange between students do take place. There are many ways to achieve this.

Taking TNN as an example, students may wish not only to broadcast or express themselves in their native languages but also in second languages. This may in fact happen soon as the Khon Kaen foreign languages faculty have already expressed the wish to develop TNN in languages other than Thai. Students may also wish to translate entire broadcasts or selected items to make them available to larger communities. Furthermore, life in Narizoma will demand of students to settle disputes as well as understand and discuss issues. All these tasks are conducted in language and will require from students to adjust their linguistic competencies appropriately. Thus language-learning needs may emerge where they previously did not exist through a collision between the task and self. Students may wish to use the collaboration of other students to help them deal with the linguistic difficulties that they encounter. They may even engage in some on-line or even off-line language courses. Less commonly taught languages would acquire a presence if only because this presence is currently refused to them on financial rather than any other grounds. The depth of students' involvement in language-related activities will be shaped by the direct needs that they experience and the forms of support available.

Students will find support structures both off-line and on-line. Off-line support will come in the form of peers or language teachers. On-line support may come in the form of dictionaries or other exploratory tools designed to enable various forms of language analysis (cf. Lian, A-P., in THIS VOLUME). A need for on-line dictionaries will grow. Students from information technology subjects may help the situation by making it their project to create software to help bridge linguistic gaps in a multitude of ways, each piece of software perhaps fulfilling a different function. Sociology students may consider enriching the sociocultural data that comes with the software. The input from native speakers would be welcome but it would come in a form that would help to problematise understandings rather than seeking to contain them in the shape of an elusive native-speaker culture (a "C1", Kramsch, 1993, p. 211). There are countless possibilities.

The key to making all these exchanges possible is the original set-up of the environment. It is believed that the technological organisation of the environment will change as Narizoma experts take over and its future form will reflect the rules of interaction as they develop in an organic fashion. In summary, Narizoma is an environment where everyone affects everyone else and where everyone can contribute in one way or another, not to mention the off-line communities which no doubt will be drawn in and affected in unpredictable ways by the on-line interactions. Thus Narizoma has the potential to create a truly integrated and integrating space.

Technological and other support in Narizoma

Technically, the Narizoma environment will be designed as a combination of various platforms. The place where people live is constructed as a 3D world (possibly using the Active Worlds software) and is completely left for students to organise as they please. Nothing prevents the Narizoma citizens from writing their own 3D software and, in the process, challenging the commercial world to create more flexible products. The learning of how to use the 3D world is left entirely up to the members of Narizoma. As Dolan's study has shown, students help one another quite eagerly to resolve whatever technical problems may arise in managing a 3D world (Dolan, 2003). In Dolan's study, after the first 10 days, most students were proficient in using the basic tools. Unlike most environments which, in one way or another, are oriented toward providing students with specific knowledge content and the means for acquiring this knowledge, the main focus of all the support structures which accompany Narizoma is different. Since dialogue happens between incommensurable positions, it can occur only when incommensurability is experienced and is driven by the objective of enhancing the degree of commensurability between them. Thus to enhance dialogic conditions, the Narizoma environment seeks to provide its citizens with tools which can help them identify incommensurable frames of reference which prevent cooperation. The idea is to enhance the degree of commensurability in order for individuals to enhance (enrich) the frames of reference in terms of which they act and interpret actions.

To this end, apart from standard communication tools which accompany most Internet-based communication platforms, Narizoma will also be equipped with a number of browsing facilities which would allow for organising interactions in ways that make them visible, thematically identifiable, and stored in such a way as to allow for 'needs-specific' exploration. Databases will play an important role here. Whatever the activities within the Narizoma, its databases should be able to store information, organise it and enable students to re-arrange it according their specific requirements. To follow the example of news/radio-broadcasts, the databases should be able to arrange the broadcasting channels according to a variety of criteria that may appear to be of value. Such criteria might include specific stations, languages, the genre of the channel and the authors. The databases may also have a facility which, for each query, would indicate the most popular similar items selected by others. Databases should be constructed which function as Narizoma libraries, storing historical and other documentation produced within the life of the community. The ways in which this information may be organised need not correspond to the systems of description currently applied in the "old world". Everything that happens in Narizoma is subject to creative negotiation. Databases should also organise information about specific research projects in the Narizoma world for others to know, and possibly join or observe. Narizoma will therefore include a number of databases and search engines, each allowing for different forms of interrogation of the dynamics of this developing world.

Not all Narizoma activities need happen within the space available to it. The databases can link Narizoma citizens to various other websites conducting activities relevant to Narizoma (like TNN). The important issue here is to create databases which integrate the contents of those sites and therefore incorporate them directly into the life of Narizoma. Databases will need to be multilingual and will have to allow for more as well as for less detailed searches. Furthermore, systems will have to be written so as to allow for the automatic storage of information and there may also be facilities for students themselves to enter information directly into databases. Allowing students to enter their own information is a very important aspect of their empowerment within Narizoma. There is an inexhaustible amount of possibilities that can help Narizoma citizens enhance their communication. The main thing is not to attempt to exhaust them but to provide a few options in the beginning for the participants, subsequently, to develop their own facilities and to control them. Finally, it is important to emphasise that technological support is not the only support available. Much support will come from the people around the participants, on- and off-line, their peers, their teachers and the community at large. Most importantly, as the TNN study showed, not all knowledge comes to us in writing.

Conclusion

This chapter took it as its goal to introduce the concept of Narizoma, a learning environment currently under development. The objectives and the structure of the environment were conceptualised in such a way as to escape the drawbacks of pedagogies which frame the learning process into following a particular path and a particular result thus reducing the possibilities of dialogue and critical exploration. Examples of such learning spaces were discussed and it was argued that environments which reinforce divisions between individuals in terms of arbitrarily selected commonalities lack in pedagogic frameworks capable of offering dialogue be it between individuals divided by language or by other socially constructed interests. The difference that the Narizoma project and its precursors (e.g. TNN) offer is their capacity to bring people together in the goal of helping one another in negotiating the means and the terms in relation to which they approach their contexts of interaction. This is the dialogue which is at stake. The objective is to maintain dialogue and in the process to grow the frames of reference in relation to which individuals evaluate and hence restructure their communicative behaviour. It is with this specific notion in mind that the concept of dialogue was used in this chapter.

It was also argued that Narizoma and TNN could support dialogue precisely because they challenge their participants to inquire about the conditions in relation to which interactions (and human relations at large) are structured, interpreted and enacted. Furthermore, these environments are likely to involve students on exploration paths which are largely unpredictable. The pedagogic and technological challenge that they issue is for the support structures provided not to limit the inquiry itself to the means available but to expand the field of inquiry beyond the immediate on-line environment. In the context of TNN therefore students were taught to explore a wide range of possibilities available to them through technology and also through the strengthening of their links with each other and with the community around them. Narizoma resolves the problem of unpredictability in a similar way. On the one hand, it provides the environment with standard communication tools and with technological assistance oriented largely toward helping the participants to sieve through information. On the other hand, it relies on human support and it is envisaged that the development of its technological support structures will build up as life in Narizoma progresses. It is this autopoietic aspect of Narizoma that can turn this vision into reality.

References

Bourdieu, P. (1991). *Language and symbolic power*, (Translated by J. B. Thompson), Cambridge, MA: Harvard University Press.

Buranapatana, M. & Lian, A. B. (2002). Thai News Network: Critical thinking in a Thai reading programs. A paper presented within the Interdisciplinary Research Seminars, University of Canberra, Australia. Retrieved December 2, 2003 from http://www.anialian.com/TNN_project.html

Calhoun, C. (2003). Ethnicity in the Cosmopolitan Imaginary. *Ethnicities*, 4. (forthcoming) Retrieved 18, April 2004 from http://www.yale.edu/polisci/info/conferences/calhoun1.doc

Calhoun, C. (2002). Information technology and the international public sphere. Paper presented to the International Sociological Association, Brisbane, Australia. Retrieved 2, December 2003 from http://www.ssrc.org/programs/calhoun/publications/infotechandpublicsphere.pdf

Chambers, R. (1996). Cultural studies as a challenge to French studies. *Australian Journal of French Studies*, 33(3), 137-156.

Cryle, P. (1996). Teaching for cultural performance. *Australian Journal of French Studies*, 33(2), 278-288.

De Nooy, J. (1996). A particularly general phenomenon? Apropos of Claire Kramsch, Context and culture in language teaching. *Australian Journal of French Studies*, 2, 204-216.

DiMaggio, P., Hargittai, E., Neuman, W. R. & Robinson, J.P. (2001). Social implications of the Internet. *Annual Review of Sociology*, 27, 307-335.

Dolan, D. (2003). Learner differences, interaction and feedback: results & implications of the initial stage of the ILE project. Paper presented at the EUROCALL 2003 conference, Limerick, Ireland.

Freadman, A. (1994). Models of genre for language teaching. Paper delivered at The Sonia Marks Memorial Lecture, University of Sydney, Sydney.

Freebody, P., Luke, A. & Gilbert, P. (1991). Reading positions and practices in the classroom. *Curriculum Inquiry*, 21(4), 435-457.

Furstenberg, G., Levet, S., English, K. & Maillet, K. (2001). Giving a virtual voice to the silent language of culture: The *Cultura* project. *Language Learning & Technology*, 5(1), 55-102. Retrieved December 1, 2003 from http://llt.msu.edu/vol5num1/furstenberg/default.pdf

Hymes, D. (1996). Ethnography, linguistics, narrative inequality. Toward an understanding of voice, London, Taylor and Francis.

Kramsch, C. (1993). *Context and culture in language teaching*. Oxford University Press.

Kramsch, C., & Thorne, S. (2002). Foreign language learning as global communicative pPractice. In Block, D. and Cameron, D. (Eds.), *Globalization and language teaching* (pp. 83-100). London: Routledge. Retrieved December 1, 2003 from http://language.la.psu.edu/~thorne/KramschThorne.html

Lantolf, J. (2000). Introducing sociocultural theory. In Lantolf, J. (Ed.), *Sociocultural theory and second language learning* (pp. 1-26). Oxford: Oxford University Press.

Latour, B. (2000). How to talk about the body? The normative dimension of science studies. First written for a symposium organized by Akrich and Berg in Paris, September 1999 *Theorizing the Body*. Revised January 2000, November 2002. Retrieved December 1, 2003 from http://www.ensmp.fr/~latour/articles/article/077.html

Latour, B. (2002). 'Why Has Critique Run out of Steam?', Retrieved April 11, 2004 from http://www.ensmp.fr/PagePerso/CSI/Bruno_Latour.html/articles/article/089.html

Lian, A-P. & Mestre, M-C. (1985). Goal-directed communicative interaction and macrosimulation. *Revue de Phonétique Appliquée*, 73-74-75, 185-210.

Lian, A-P. (2004). Technology-enhanced language-learning: A rhizomatic approach. In this volume.

Thorne, S. (2003). Artifacts and cultures-of-use in intercultural communication. *Language Learning & Technology*, 7(2), 38-67.

Tripp, D. (1992). Critical theory and educational research. *Issues In Educational Research*, 2(1), 13-23. Retrieved December 1, 2003 from http://education.curtin.edu.au/iier/iier2/tripp.html

3

MOO virtual worlds in CMC-based CALL: Defining an agenda for future research

Mark Peterson

Abstract

The expanding use of computers has led to changes in the nature of education in the 21st century. All spheres of education have been influenced by this phenomenon and there has been a burgeoning interest in the application of computers in the language classroom. At the same time new areas of research have emerged, focusing on the impact of new technology on applied linguistics. Advances in network technologies have fostered the development of many novel tools including online virtual environments known as MOOs (multi-user object-orientated domains). These environments are designed to facilitate text-based synchronous communication and content creation within the context of a virtual world. A number of MOOs have been developed for use in second language education. In this context developments in second language acquisition (SLA) and computer-mediated communication (CMC) research, have emphasized the important role of interaction and collaboration in learners' interlanguage development. This chapter examines the findings of studies into the application of MOO environments in computer-assisted language learning (CALL). Drawing on this literature, this chapter explores the various theoretical and pedagogical issues associated with the application of these tools in second language education. In conclusion, the discussion will highlight areas of potential for future research.

Introduction

Of the many new developments in CALL, one of the most promising areas requiring investigation is the application of synchronous communications tools in the language classroom. Studies have reported on the application of conferencing software and Internet chat programs in foreign language writing instruction (Kelm, 1992, Kern, 1995; Warschauer, 1996a). However many other aspects of the application of these tools in language learning remain largely unexplored. Of the many Internet communications tools currently being utilized in CALL research, increasing interest has focused on multi-user object-orientated domain (MOO)-based learning.

MOOs have attracted attention from researchers as they bring together diverse groups of learners in structured collaborative environments, focusing on interaction in the target language (TL). MOOs further provide a sense of permanence and community that is often lacking in other forms of chat environment (Kotter, 2003). Thus in some respects, learning in MOOs conforms to current constructs in second language acquisition research that stress the role of meaningful interaction and the social context of learning (Peterson, 2001). This chapter will describe these environments and attempt an overview of studies on their use in CALL, with the intention of providing directions for research in this area.

MOO-based learning environments

MOOs are virtual environments designed to facilitate text-based synchronous communication between users via networks. Most MOOs are accessible via telnet or in some cases through a web browser. There are a number of differences between MOOs and other forms of synchronous chat tool. In contrast to conventional chat programs, these environments are designed around a hierarchy of user privileges that enables the creators of a MOO to structure the environment to meet the needs of specific learner groups. This feature enables users with appropriate privileges to utilize object-oriented programming (a unique element of MOOs) in order to create, manipulate and share multimedia objects and applications. Unlike transient chat rooms, user-created rooms and other forms of content are permanent in MOOs and can be edited and extended at any time. Many MOOs also offer a number of features not found in many conventional chat programs including a mailing system, logging functions and special objects including tape recorders and VCRs. A further novel aspect of MOOs is their spatial metaphor. In MOOs learners can traverse virtual space within a fully featured virtual world that incorporates graphical maps and other navigation aids. Navigation is achieved through the use of a specific set of MOO-specific commands or in the case of web-based MOOs mouse clicks.

Many MOOs designed for language learners contain extensive online help pages and archives. MOOs adopt various learning metaphors such as for example, a virtual university making possible the creation of online learning environments that engender a higher degree of permanence, collaboration and sense of community than other forms of synchronous chat.

MOOs may be accessed through a web browser or through a client program such as telnet. Accessing MOOs is a relatively simple process. MOO environments require that users log in, by completing a simple log in protocol. Users may log in as guests, however MOOs are designed to encourage the adoption of a character nickname or alias. The use of pseudonyms provides for anonymity (Von der Emde, Schneider, & Kotter, 2001), prevents abuse of the medium (as abusive users may be removed from the environment) and in many cases fosters the development of an on-line persona on the part of users (Turkle, 1996). This aspect of MOOs sustains the high levels of learner participation that are characteristic of many CALL projects involving MOOs (Kotter, 2003). (A screen capture of a gateway interface for a language learning MOO is reproduced below):

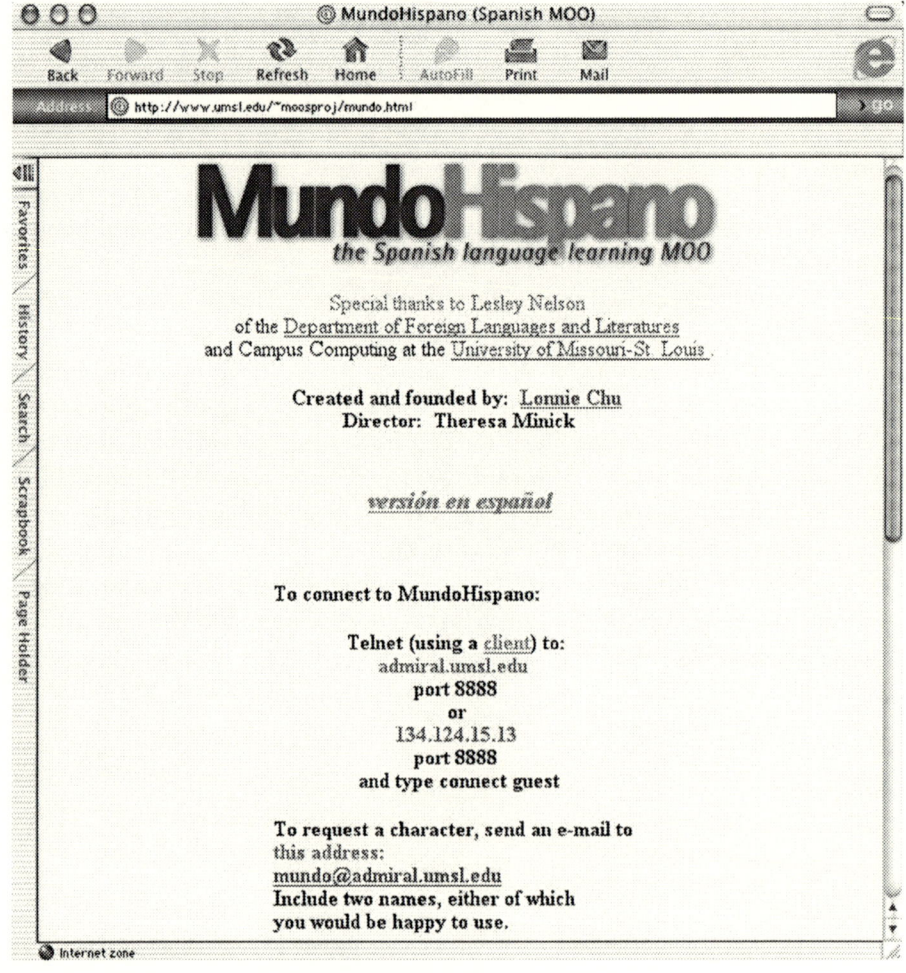

Figure 1 A MOO gateway interface (reproduced by permission of Lonnie Chu)

On completion of this protocol users are then free to communicate, navigate and manipulate virtual objects within the MOO by means of a series of mouse clicks or text-based commands. An example of learner generated MOO discourse involving a discussion of multiculturalism is reproduced below (Von der Emde et al., 2001, p. 221):

Barbara says: "integration is as important and…wait just a second"
Luigi [to Barbara] : And we don't have any umlauts, don't forget

Sarah says, " I think that integration is the same as "assimilate"
Barbara [to Luiji] : How?
Sarah says, "What I am confused!"
Barbara [to Sarah]: They aren't, I think, the same thing.
Barbara [to Sarah] : Why?
Sarah says, "Peraps they are not quite the same"
Luigi says, "Assimilate sounds like an attack [Angriff], integrate sounds friendlier in any case"
Barbara [to Sarah] : I'm going to just check the dictionary. I'll be right back.
Sarah says, "Integrate means that the people can live together"
Sarah says, "Angriff?"
Luigi says, "Oh, I am thinking of assimilate from Star Trek (You will be assimilated)"
Sarah [to Luigi]: oohhh
Luigi says, "Are assimilate and integrate the same thing in America?"
Barbara says, "The dictionary says that they are translations of each other, but I don't understand them as the same"
Sarah says, "Do you think that when people are integrated thay have to lose their identity?"

On obtaining a certain level of user privilege, learners may also create virtual spaces and objects within a MOO. MOO environments are based on these user-created spaces known as rooms. Typically MOOs contain numerous virtual rooms, linked together by entrances and exists. Most language learning MOOs contain large numbers of these learner created rooms, designed to facilitate discussion on various themes. The following screen capture shows a learner produced virtual room in an ESL MOO.

44   Mark Peterson

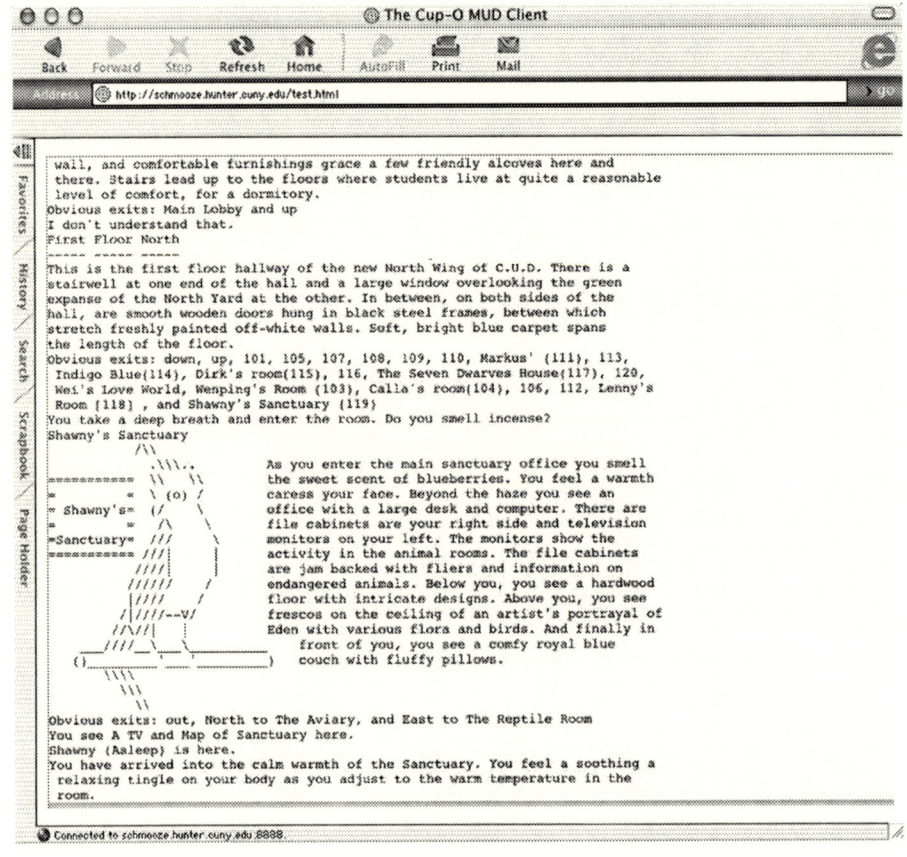

Figure 2 An ESL MOO virtual room (reproduced by permission of Julie Falsetti)

Some MOO environments contain numerous learning objects including virtual projectors, lecture spaces, notes, web pages and recording devices. Recent browser-based MOOs also provide access to a number of authoring tools that enable users to create, share and edit virtual objects and applications (Haynes & Holmevik, 2001). An example of a hypertext MOO interface is reproduced below:

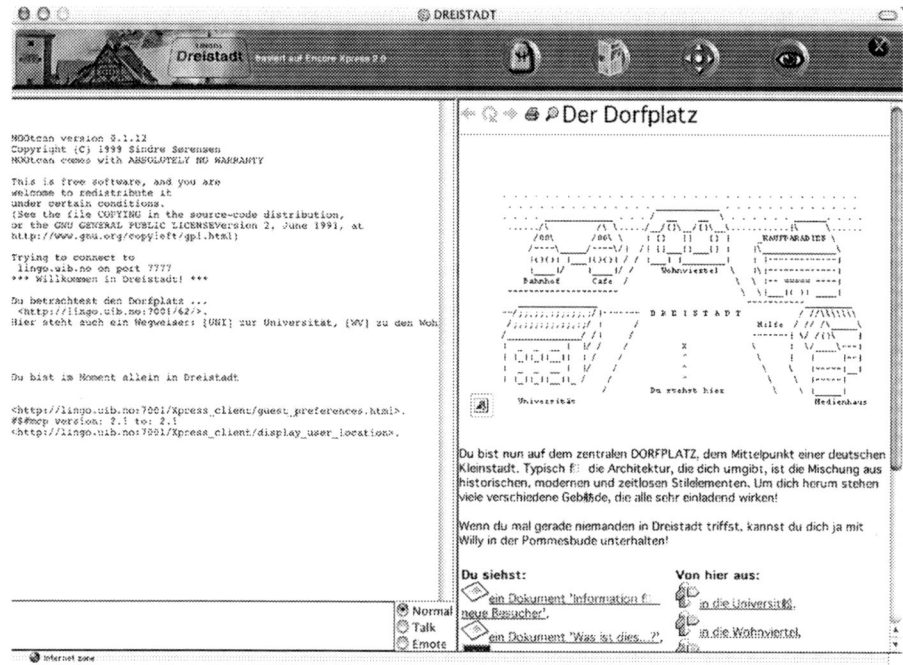

Figure 3 A hypermedia MOO interface (reproduced by permission of Daniel Jung)

Although browser-based MOOs have only been utilized in CALL relatively recently and are still under active development, researchers have not been slow to see the potential benefits of learning in these environments. In recent years, increasing numbers of language learning MOOs have been developed for a number of languages. A number of preliminary studies on the use of MOOs in CALL have been conducted (Donaldson & Kotter 1999b; Kotter, 2003; Von der Emde, et al., 2001) and their results suggest a number of positive effects on learners L2 development. The following section will focus on a discussion of these studies.

The current literature on MOOs in CALL

The findings of several studies suggest that participation in MOO based learning may have the potential to enhance language acquisition processes (Donaldson and Kotter, 1999a; Kotter, 2003; Schwienhorst 2002; Schwienhorst, 1997; Von der Emde, et al., 2001). Current research identifies several areas where positive results have been achieved. These benefits are similar to the hypothesized benefits of CMC and in addition there appear to be other areas where the unique features of MOOs may be utilized to the benefit of learners.

Studying in MOOs shares many of the advantages of learning in other CMC environments. These factors include the removal of traditional constraints on learning such as time and distance (Harasim, 1996). Moreover as with learning in many of the synchronous environments that do not encompass video and audio technologies, MOOs provide anonymity and remove the visual and aural cues that may inhibit reticent learners (Hudson & Bruckman, 2002), and those disadvantaged in traditional classrooms (Warschauer, Turbee & Roberts, 1996). The distributed nature of learner activities in synchronous CMC environments such as MOOs also provides for a wider range of interactions than are possible in conventional classrooms (Kitade, 2000).

As with many types of synchronous environment utilized in CALL, learning in MOOs may also promote more equal participation as wait times are reduced. In addition the online nature of interaction in synchronous CMC results in the removal of turn taking pressures (Crystal, 2001, p.148), leading to the possibility of increased linguistic output (Ortega, 1997).

As with some other forms of synchronous CMC used in CALL, learning in MOOs leads to a beneficial restructuring of conventional classroom dynamics. A study by Donaldson and Kotter (1999a) found that in a MOO-based tandem learning project involving college students studying German in America and adult ESL students in Germany, learners took increased responsibility for their learning. This phenomenon became more pronounced, as this five month project progressed.

In a pilot project involving learners in Germany and Ireland described by Schwienhorst (1997), similar behaviors were observed and the real time nature of communication in MOOs supported learner motivation and participation. The above studies also highlight a further significant feature of MOO-based projects described in the literature. Participation in CMC-based learning appears to engineer a shift in the dynamics of learning away from traditional teacher-led modalities. As no participant can dominate the floor in synchronous discussion (due to the fact that in online environments such as MOOs the influence of affective factors is removed), the application of CMC environments in CALL has led to a reconceptualisation of the role of the teacher. In several MOO projects the role of teacher changed from that of instructor to facilitator (Donaldson & Kotter, 1999a, Shield, Weininger, & Davies, 1999b). While the authors of the above studies (Donaldson & Kotter, 1999a, Shield et al., 1999a) viewed this change positively, these developments have implications for the future of pedagogy given the increasing use of online learning in language education. The issues raised by this development will be discussed in a later section of this paper.

In the context of MOO-based learning, a number of authors have noted a further positive aspect of learning in these environments, the creation of dynamic communities of learning focused on task-based pedagogies (Becker, 2001, Shield Weininger, & Davies, 1999a). In a semester long study conducted at Vassar College, a group of students in America studying German as a second language were paired with a group of native speakers of German based in Germany (Von der Emde, et al., 2001). The project was characterized by a high degree of authentic learner centered communication. As the project progressed the researchers noted the emergence of extensive peer teaching and autonomous learning behaviors. This phenomenon appears to be fostered by the egalitarian nature of much online discourse.

Echoing these findings several studies have indicated that learning in MOOs supports the development of learner autonomy (Shield et al., 1999b, Schwienhorst, 1997). Authors of a number of studies have noted that MOO-based environments foster peer teaching and collaborative learning (Shield et al., 1999b, Von der Emde, et al., 2001). This has led some researchers to claim (Shield et al., 1999b) that as these environments bring together groups of learners for cooperative interaction, they may conform to the Vygotskyan notions of the optimal learning environment (Vygotsky, 1978).

A further area where MOO-based learning may support L2 development lies in the area of interaction. Studies involving MOO projects indicate that most discourse is learner-generated and conducted primarily in the TL (Donaldson & Kotter 1999b; Schwienhorst 1997; Von der Emde, et al., 2001). These findings indicate that learning in MOO environments in many cases, provides learners with access to comprehensible input. Moreover these studies also provide evidence to suggest that the synchronous nature of interaction in MOOs, may promote the kind of pushed interaction (Long 1996) that is held to facilitate the development of L2 competences. Participation in MOO-based projects may therefore provide learners with opportunities to produce increasingly complex modified output (Von der Emde, et al., 2001). This aspect of learning in MOOs may be facilitated when interaction is focused around authentic tasks (Peterson, 2001). The provision of opportunities for the kind of meaning-focused purposeful interaction held to be influential in current interactionist views of SLA, has recently been hypothesized as a major element of a rationale for the use of MOOs in CALL (Peterson, 2001). Significantly a recent study by Schwienhorst (2002) has found that participation in a MOO-based CALL project stimulated the development of discourse repair strategies on the part of learners. This study suggests that learning in MOOs provides an instructional context that provides opportunities for the kind of interaction that promotes interlanguage development. The following table presents the key findings of the studies discussed in this section.

Table 1. Hypothesized advantages of utilizing MOOs in CALL

Advantage	Study
Removal of time and distance constraints	Harasim 1996
Absence of audiovisual cues benefits reticent learners and those from traditionally disadvantaged learner groups	Hudson & Bruckman 2002 Warschauer et al. 1996b
Opportunities to create personally meaningful artifacts	Shield et al. 1999a
The development of metacognitive skills such as noticing	Kotter 2003
Development of discourse management skills	Pinto 1999
Access to a wider range of interlocutors than are found in conventional classrooms	Kitade 2000
Change in classroom dynamics (move towards learner-focused classrooms)	Donaldson & Kotter 1999a
Opportunities for collaborative learning and the development of cross cultural understanding	Von der Emde et al. 2001
Opportunities to implement task-based pedagogies	Peterson 2001
Opportunities to foster the development of learner autonomy, exploratory learning and language play	Schwienhorst 1997 Shield et al. 1999b Von der Emde et al. 2001
Production of modified output	Pellettieri 2000
Opportunities to engage in the negotiation of meaning	Schwienhorst 2002 Kotter 2003

MOO environments: Unique features

In addition to the above aspects of network-based learning that MOOs share with other CMC environments, there are a number of novel features of MOOs that may be utilized to support the development of second language learning competences. One of the significant advantages that MOOs provide over other modes of CMC is that MOO environments enable learners to create personally meaningful learning objects, including virtual discussion spaces and multimedia content. This form of activity in MOOs facilitates learning, by providing a sense of ownership and also enables learners to actively collaborate in the production of new knowledge. This form of learning is held to be a powerful form of scaffolding (Shield et al., 1999a).

Moreover MOO environments are more structured than many other forms of CMC. In contrast to the transient nature of many Internet chat rooms, most language learning MOOs have been extensively developed by learners themselves to create permanent structured virtual spaces incorporating virtual rooms and content. Unlike most chat rooms the level of functionality available to a user in a MOOs is determined by a hierarchy of user privilege. Progression to the highly levels of user privilege is based on the acceptance of a set of explicit MOO-specific criteria provided by the owner of the MOO. This aspect of MOOs facilitates the creation of orderly virtual communities based on the acceptance of well defined behavioral norms. The structured format of MOO worlds lends itself more readily to task-based pedagogies than most other forms of synchronous CMC. Task-based pedagogies have been implemented in a number of MOO projects with encouraging results (Donaldson & Kotter, 1999b, Von der Emde, et al., 2001).

The tendency of CMC environments to foster the creation of linguistic communities has been noted by a number of authors (Crystal, 2001). Several studies have noted that participation in MOO projects engenders a strong sense of community between participants (Donaldson & Kotter, 1999a, Von der Emde, et al., 2001). This aspect of participation in MOO-based learning appears to support the development of friendships and the creation of dynamic communities of learning (Donaldson & Kotter, 1999b) to a greater degree that has been found in other forms of synchronous CMC environment utilized in CALL. While this aspect of MOO based learning has yet to be studied extensively, the social nature of learning in MOOs has led a number of researchers to speculate that learning in MOOs may create conditions supportive to learners' second language development (Schwienhorst, 2002, Shield et al., 1999b). From the constructivist perspective MOO environments have great potential as learning tools, as they enable learners to socially construct new knowledge.

A further beneficial aspect of the high degree of learner collaboration that characterizes many MOO projects, is the positive effects that this form of interaction has on the development of learners cross-cultural understanding and knowledge of the TL culture. Several researchers (e.g., Donaldson & Kotter, 1999a; Donaldson & Kotter, 1999b; Von der Emde et al., 2001) have observed that as MOOs facilitate interaction between a wide range of learner groups they provide a more culturally diverse learning experience than may be found in many conventional classrooms. This view leads to the hypothesis that the experience of learning in real time with interlocutors from other cultures has the effect of broadening learners' cross cultural understanding and knowledge of a TL culture. The literature indicates that this tendency may be more pronounced in international MOO projects involving native speaker participants (Donaldson & Kotter, 1999b). By bringing together diverse learner groups for purposeful interaction current research indicates that MOO environments have the potential to act as powerful tools to support the development of cross-cultural communication and communicative competency (Kotter, 2003).

The permanence of the written medium also provides further benefits to learning in MOOs. In MOOs learner output is available on screen as it is produced, thus providing immediate feedback. Learners may also scroll back in order to consider their responses to interlocutors (Shield et al., 1999b). Learner interaction in MOOs can be recorded in "log files". The study of these logs by learners has been used in a number of MOO projects to promote metacognitive skills such as noticing (Donaldson & Kotter, 1999a) and awareness of conversation management techniques (Pinto, 1999, p. 182). Furthermore, as all learner interaction in MOOs is conducted in text, learners can participate in peer review and other reflective learning activities (Shield et al., 1999a). In addition, the anonymous textual nature of interaction in MOOs also provides learners with opportunities to indulge in exploratory learning and language play, activities seen as important in the development of learners' L2 proficiencies (Von der Emde et al., 2001).

As the above discussion illustrates, the applicant of MOO environments in language education raises a number of important research issues. The remainder of this paper will focus on a discussion of a number of promising areas for future research.

Areas for future research

The application of CMC-based environments such as MOOs in CALL provides researchers with a unique opportunity to examine the nature of a new dynamic form of language and may also provide new insights into the complex nature of online learning. Future research efforts into the use of CMC and MOOs in language education will focus on a number of key areas. The first of these will be an examination from a linguistic and interactionist perspective, of the language produced in CMC environments.

The language of CMC

In a recent book Crystal (2002), has characterized the language of the Internet as a new variety of written language. In the context of CMC-based CALL the extensive use by learners of a unique register that encompasses partial sentences, invented words and iconic symbols appears to confirm this observation (Chapelle, 2000, Collot & Belmore, 1996). If this is indeed the case, the study of the language produced in online environments such as MOOs will yield many insights into this new form of communication. From the perspective of interactionist research it has further been suggested that CALL projects that utilize synchronous CMC may promote L2 competencies as these environments bring together effectively, the interactive nature of conversation with the reflective aspects of writing (Warschauer, 1996b).

A recent paper by Peterson (2001), speculates that participation in MOO-based projects may provide learners with opportunities to take part in the process of negotiation. Studies by Schwienhorst (2002) and Kotter (2003) have shown that learners involved in MOO-based collaborative learning projects engaged in the kind of interactional moves (clarification requests, comprehension and confirmation checks) and repairs associated with negotiation. Future projects that utilize the data recording capacities of MOO environments will contribute to the investigation of these claims. While learner interaction in MOOs has yet to be comprehensibly investigated, the interactionist perspective does highlight the general need for extensive quantitative studies into the discourse produced by learners in CMC environments such as MOOs.

From an interactionist perspective future studies may focus on significant issues such as the lexical range and syntactic complexity of learners' linguistic output in CMC. Researchers adopting an interactionist perspective will also examine learner behaviour in CMC-based CALL. In the future, this work could be carried out with a view to establishing a linkage between the various types of CMC and the development of particular L2 competences. Such studies will provide a valuable body of data that may facilitate the future investigation of the effects of variables such as task, age and proficiency levels on possible linguistic development in CMC. Qualitative investigations based on observational data including learner reports, think aloud protocols and questionnaires will shed new light on research issues that are as yet largely unexplored. Issues requiring investigation also include the role of affective variables such as learner differences and strategies in CMC-based CALL. The study of learner interaction in CMC further raises major issues regarding the development of CALL research and language teaching pedagogy.

CMC or SLA research: A basis for future development in CALL?

The emergence of CMC-based CALL also highlights a major issue with regard to the conflicting views of the future development of CALL. Contemporary CALL research stresses the need to develop a coherent and principled theoretical base (Levy, 1997), however opinions vary with regard to the role of CMC in the development of CALL as a systematic research field. Some have argued that the best way to develop CALL as a discipline is to view CMC as merely one aspect of CALL research (Chapelle, 1997). From this perspective, research activities in CALL should draw on current interactionist research paradigms (Chapelle, 2000). Supporters of the alternative view claim that the emergence of CMC-based CALL requires a radical evaluation of current conceptions of CALL research. These researchers argue that while interactionist models of SLA are useful in acquisition related CALL research, there is a need to develop a wider range of constructs that emphasize the diverse and salient aspects of computer mediated learning (Harrington & Levy, 2001).

This viewpoint perceives that CMC-based interaction is a new form of interaction that is also qualitatively and quantitatively different from face-to-face communication. Given the limited amount of research conducted in this area the above debate will continue for some time. However their remains a clear need to undertake studies from a number of perspectives in order to advance our understanding of the nature of CMC, SLA and their possible role in the future of CALL research (Warschauer, 1998). The above debate also raises a further important issue with regard to the application of CMC in CALL, namely the role of pedagogy in networked learning environments.

CMC and language teaching pedagogy

The application in CALL of CMC environments such as MOOs raises a number of issues with regard to current pedagogy. A central focus of future pedagogical development in CMC-based CALL will doubtless be the investigation of the nature and role of tasks in supporting learners' second language development. From an interactionist perspective, a study by Pellettieri (2000) claims that interaction in CMC follows many of the patterns that are found in face-to-face communication. In the context of tasks, the significant findings of this study included the fact that lexical items and content factors trigged the great majority of negotiations. In addition, tasks that contained form focused components resulted in a higher level of negotiation at the morphosyntactic level. Moreover challenging closed activities created more negotiation than other types of task. Although these findings are preliminary in nature, they have clear implications for the design of tasks in CMC-based learning.

The significant changes in classroom dynamics reported in several studies further suggests that teaching using CMC technologies may led to a significant reconceptualisation of traditional teacher and learner roles (Peterson, 1997). The technology supported classrooms of the future may in many cases, require learners to become active participants in the learning process. In this context some research suggests that the use of CMC environments in CALL requires the development of new pedagogies for learning with technology that are a departure from the behaviorist models that remain influential (Warschauer et al., 1996). While a consensus is yet to emerge on this issue, future research in this area may attempt to re-evaluate language teaching pedagogy in networked classroom contexts. This effort may involve exploring how the potential advantages offered by CMC technologies can be applied in a pedagogically appropriate manner to the benefit of learners.

Table 2. Areas for future research on MOOs in CALL

Research question	Research approach
What is the discourse status of MOO-based CMC?	Discourse analysis
Does negotiation occur in MOO-based CMC?	Quantitative studies
What kind of pedagogies can be developed to support learning in MOOs?	Qualitative studies
What are the influences of affective variables on MOO-based CALL?	Qualitative studies

Conclusion

This chapter has attempted to demonstrate that the application of MOOs in CALL is an important area for future linguistic research. The existing literature highlights the urgent need for more extensive studies in order to increase our understanding of what may be one of the most promising recent developments in the field. An examination of the past history of CALL development highlights the value of adopting a systematic approach in this endeavor. If progress is to be made, then clearly this research effort should be based on the coordinated collection of a systematic body of work. Given the interdisciplinary nature of research in CMC-based CALL, researchers in the future can adopt a variety of perspectives in order to broaden our understanding of this new and dynamic field. Moreover, the increasing use of CMC in all its forms has major implications for pedagogy. There remains a need to develop innovative pedagogies in order to fully utilize the educational potential of MOOs and other CMC environments. The study of CMC environments such as MOOs offers researchers a unique opportunity to observe learner interaction and the development of a new form of language and communication. Future studies will enable researchers to develop a fuller understanding of the potential of these environments as language learning tools and also illuminate the complex interaction between language, technology and learning in CMC environments.

References

Backer, J. (2001,May). Using a modular approach to schMOOze with ESL/EFL students. *The Internet TESL Journal, 8*(5). Retrieved June 25, 2004 from http://iteslj.org/Lessons/Backer-SchMOOze.html

Chapelle, C. A. (1997). CALL in the year 2000: Still in search of research paradigms? *Language Learning and Technology, 1*(1), 19-43.

Chapelle, C. A. (2000). Is network-based learning CALL? In M. Warschauer & R. Kern (Eds.), *Network-based language teaching: Concepts and Practice* (pp. 204-228). Cambridge: Cambridge University Press.

Collot, M., & Belmore, N. (1996). Electronic language: A new variety of English. In S. C. Herring (Ed.), *Computer-mediated communication: Linguistic, social and cross-cultural perspectives* (pp. 13-28). Amsterdam: Benjamins.

Crystal, D. (2002). *Language and the Internet.* Cambridge: Cambridge University Press.

Donaldson, R. P., & Kotter, M. (1999a). Language learning in a MOO: Creating a transoceanic bilingual virtual community. *Literary and Linguistic Computing, 14*(1), 67-76.

Donaldson, R. P., & Kotter, M. (1999b). Language learning in cyberspace: Teleporting the classroom into the target language culture. *Calico, 16*(4), 531-557.

Harrington, M. & Levy, M. (2001). CALL begins with a "C": Interaction in computer-mediated language learning. *System, 29*(1), 15-26.

Harasim, L. (1986). Computer learning networks: Educational applications of computer conferencing. *Journal of Distance Education, 1*(1), 59-70.

Haynes, C., & Holmevik, J. R. (Eds.), (2001). *High wired: On the design, use, and theory of educational MOOs.* Ann Arbour: The University of Michigan Press.

Hudson, J. M. & Bruckman, A. S. (2002). IRC Français: The creation of an Internet-based SLA community. *Computer Assisted Language Learning, 15*(2), 109-134.

Kelm, O.R. (1992). The use of synchronous computer networks in second language instruction: A preliminary report. *Foreign Language Annals, 25*(5), 441-545.

Kern, R. G. (1995). Restructuring classroom interaction with network computers: Effects on quantity and characteristics of language production. *The Modern Language Journal, 79,* 457-476.

Kitade, K. (2000). L2 learners' discourse and SLA theories in CMC: Collaborative interaction in Internet chat. *Computer Assisted Language Learning, 13*(2),143-166.

Kotter, M. (2003). Negotiation of meaning and code switching in online tandems. *Language Learning and Technology, 7*(2), 145-172.

Levy, M. (1997). *Computer-assisted language learning: Context and conceptualization.* Oxford: Clarendon Press.

Long, M.H. (1996). The role of linguistic environment in second language acquisition. In W.C. Richie & T.K. Bhatia (Eds.), *Handbook of research on language acquisition. Vol. 2: Second language acquisition* (pp. 413-468). New York: Academic Press.

Ortega, L. (1997). Processes and outcomes in networked classroom interaction: Defining the research agenda for L2 computer-assisted classroom discussion. *Language Learning & Technology, 1*(1), 82-93.

Pellettieri, J. (2000). Negotiation in cyberspace: The role of chatting in the development of grammatical competence. In R. Kern & M. Warschauer (Eds.), *Network-based language teaching: Concepts and practice* (pp. 59-86). Cambridge: Cambridge University Press.

Peterson, M. (2001). MOOs and second language acquisition: Towards a rationale for MOO-based learning. *Computer Assisted Language Learning, 14*(5), 443-459.

Peterson, M. (1997). Language teaching and networking. *Computer Assisted Language Learning, 25*(1), 29-37.

Pinto, D. (1996). What does "SchMOOze Mean?". In M. Warschauer, (Ed.), *Telecollboration in foreign language learning* (pp. 165-184). Hawaii: University of Hawaii Press.

Schwienhorst, K. (2002). Evaluating tandem learning in the MOO: Discourse repair strategies in a bilingual Internet project. *Computer Assisted Language Learning, 16*(2), 135-145.

Schwienhorst, K. (1997). *Talking on the MOO: Learner autonomy and language learning in tandem.* Paper presented at the CALLMOO: Enhancing language learning through Internet technologies, Bergen, Norway.

Schwienhorst, K. (1998). The "third place"-virtual reality applications for second language learning. *ReCALL, 10*(1), 118-126.

Shield, L.,Weininger, M. J. & Davies, L. B. (1999a). A task-based approach to using MOO for collaborative language learning. In K. Cameron (Ed.), *CALL and the learning community* (pp. 391-401). Exeter: Elm Bank Publications.

Shield, L.,Weininger, M. J. & Davies, L. B., (1999b, October). MOOing in L2: Constructivism and developing learner autonomy for technology-enhanced language learning. *C@lling Japan Online.* Retrieved November 15, 2002, from: http://jaltcall.org/cjo/10_99/

Turkle, S. (1996). *Life on the screen.* New York: Simon and Schuster.

Von der Emde, S., Schneider, J., & Kotter, M., (2001). Technically speaking: Transforming learning through virtual learning environments (MOOs). *The Modern Language Journal, 85*(2), 210-225.

Vygotsky, L. (1978). *Mind and Society.* Cambridge: Harvard University Press.

Warschauer, M. (1996a). Comparing face-to-face and electronic discussion in the second language classroom. *CALICO Journal, 13*, 7-25.

Warschauer, M. (1996b). *Computer-mediated collaborative learning: Theory and practice.* (Research note 17). University of Hawaii.

Warschauer, M. (1998). Interaction, negotiation, and computer-mediated learning. In M. Clay (Ed.), *Practical applications of educational technology in language learning*. Lyon, France: National Institute of Applied Sciences. Retrieved November 15, 2002 from: http://www.insalyon.fr/Departements/CDRL/interaction.html

Warschauer, M., Turbee, L. & Roberts, B. (1996). Computer learning networks and student empowerment. *System, 24*(1), 1-14.

4

CALL initiatives and the Korean cultural learning context

David Kent

Abstract

Historic reforms initiated in the education system throughout the 1990s, combined with efforts to secure the pervasiveness of information communication technology (ICT) in the nation over the last decade, are starting to greatly impact the life of every South Korean. Various details of these impacts are presented, including the ways in which South Korean educators are applying computer-assisted language learning (CALL). However, despite the increasing use of CALL and multimedia applications within the education sector at large, it is highlighted that the use of computer-based technology for teaching at the tertiary level is practically non-existent within mandatory English language programs or individual native-speaker classes. An inquiry is also conducted into how the pervasiveness of Confucian consciousness in South Korea influences both the classrooms of native-speakers as well as the ways in which South Korean EFL (English as a Foreign Language) students approach the use of CALL. A need to take the importance of the local cultural context and learning environment into account, when teaching and learning with CALL initiatives, is then emphasised. Further, attention is drawn to areas where research is lacking in the South Korean CALL and EFL arenas.

Introduction

In the digital era the need to educate an increasing number of people within South Korea, hereafter Korea, has led to both bold reforms and experimentation with advanced technologies (I. Jung, 2000). Recent reforms include the widespread development and integration of ICT, restructuring of the college scholastic ability test (CSAT), focus on student-centred education, and increased English language teaching. However, as Park and Oxford (1998) state, Korea is racially homogenous and primarily monolingual. Consequently students have little opportunity to use English outside classrooms, and although technology increases access to English learning contexts it is not as interactive as students need. Although Jeon and Kim (2001) have pointed out that Korean education is undergoing an historic change, and communicative-competence is gaining focus in English classrooms, it is apparent that "students have little access to authentic language input and limited opportunities to interact with native speakers" (S. Y. Kim, 2002b, p. 132). The constant obstacle for EFL educators is that English is employed as a foreign language and restricted largely to classroom settings. In addition, Korean students approach native-speaker teachers through Korean cultural perspectives (Windle, 2003), and remnants of the Confucian consciousness in terms of education, and learning culture, still strongly impinge upon learning styles and teaching methods (Gray, 1998; Min, et al., 2000; Shaffer, 2001; Lim & Griffith, 2003). The impact that such perspectives have on the implementation of initiatives such as CALL is important to consider. Considering such cultural paradigms may be instructive as well as holding answers for the effective use and development of educational technology across a variety of settings.

The aim of this study is to highlight the complex relationship between the local cultural context and the implementation of educational technology by looking closely at the Korean EFL environment. This will be achieved by firstly providing an overview of the current state of EFL and ICT in the Korean education system; secondly, briefly highlighting the means by which CALL systems have been applied in the nation's EFL classrooms; then finally, considering the Confucian consciousness and illustrating one approach to employ CALL-based learning content—an approach that takes into account aspects of the Korean cultural learning style as it relates to Confucianism.

The state of EFL and ICT in the Korean education system

Throughout the 1990s education policy changes were significantly historic, especially "in the area of English teaching, [where] the decade of [the] 1990's experienced more changes than the century that had preceded it" (Kwon, 2000, p. 47). Korea today is also said to have, in terms of ICT use, one of the most advanced education strategies in Asia (UNESCO, 2002). The latest package of reforms also seeks to move education away from a teacher-centred and grade-point centred system to one providing a more student-centred approach. This goal requires an increase in elective courses and a reduction in required courses. Student-centred education thereby refers to creating a streamlined curriculum providing greater course options, where each grade school is given autonomy over the implementation of elements of the 7th National Curriculum.

The grade school environment

During the mid 90's the English Program in Korea (EPIK) was introduced into middle schools, seeing native-speakers provide education alongside Korean co-teachers, and in 1997 English was introduced as a regular subject within elementary schools. English language education then became a compulsory subject for ten years of consecutive schooling (Lee, 2001). In addition, authorized texts for third- and fourth-graders were accompanied by video and audio cassettes, while for fourth- and fifth-graders computer-based CD-ROM materials could be used.

From 2001 computer education classes for at least an hour per week have been mandatory for grades one and two, and include grades three through six in 2003. This is in addition to the use of computers for in-class instruction, and results in three to four hours of school computer exposure each week. Efforts are also underway to ensure an increase in school internet connection speeds to 2mbps and, by 2005, the assignment of one PC to at least five children per class. Currently, however, implementation of computer-based instruction for at least 10% of class time is mandatory (KERIS, 2001). Such extensive computer use has been criticized, since it can reduce other educational needs and may adversely come to impact intellectual development (M. Lee, 2001), and "not only subtracts from important developmental tasks but may also entrench bad learning habits, leading to poor motivation and even symptoms of learning disability" (Healy cited in Cuban, 2001, p. 60). H. Chun (2002) also highlights the need to question how useful and effective this material is over the video and audio content previously applied.

In terms of English language education, introduction of the 7th National Curriculum at primary and middle school levels in 2001, extended to high schools in 2003, has since seen the language offered at various levels. The curriculum also emphasizes communicative competence and fluency through a grammatical-functional syllabus (Kwon, 2000), stresses the need to understand Western culture, and as already highlighted places emphasis on computer use across all grades (K. C. Jeong, 2002). In addition, from March 2001, elementary and middle school teachers have been required to teach English through English. The most frequent problems encountered by teachers trying to implement a communicative language teaching approach in the classroom centre on the lack of teachers' English language proficiency and training in the use of communicative language teaching approaches (Li, 1998). Teachers employing this approach also report difficulties stemming from low student motivation, limited student oral proficiency and, particularly for high school teachers, large class sizes, lack of preparation time, and pressure to prepare students for the CSAT (S. Y. Kim, 2002a). In the past, emphasis placed on the CSAT resulted in distorting education to that of a test-driven nature, but from 2005 the CSAT will reflect characteristics of the new education program. This will provide an integrative approach that allows students to concentrate on courses of interest that suit their future goals, and reduce the exam preparation burden on students by acting as only one factor in a range of selection requirements for university entrance (J. Y. Park, 2002).

The university environment

During the 1990s "'Globalization' [became] one of the most popular words in Korean society" (Park, 1998, p. 123), and since the globalization campaign learning English has become one of the most important things for Korea (Kwon, 2000). This has seen employment of native English speakers as the main means to provide such training, particularly in both the cram school and tertiary education sectors. Lee (2001) comments, "educational administrators as well as our students are often misdirected to believe that native speakers are…their only resource for improving their English proficiency" (para. 11). Universities have also come to require certain pass grades on standardized English language tests, as well as proficiency in computer literacy, before students are granted graduate status. English language skills, and more recently ICT skills as well, are therefore viewed as essential.

However, in contrast to the grade school setting where computer-based initiatives are used to assist learning, government reforms for the development of ICT utilization within higher education focus firmly on administrative use, infrastructure development, and the promotion of research (KERIS, 2001). This implies a lack of focus on the development of e-learning initiatives in Korea as opposed to other nations, including regional ones like China and Japan, since tertiary education providers globally have been increasing online instruction of traditional taught courses over the last decade (Elgort, Marshall, & Mitchell, 2003). Even though cyber-class systems do exist in Korea, there is minimal CALL use within university EFL classes; systems generally lack the e-learning abilities of more advanced software, and are designed largely for classroom management support and administrative duties. These systems are predominantly web-based, and most native English speaking faculty members are locked out of their use due to lack of administrative support or problems in dealing with the Korean language interface. Subsequently, there is currently no complete alignment among universities, regarding CALL, with that of the initiatives being set in place at the grade-school level. Further, "textbooks are preferred in university-level curriculum", and "in spite of the availability and accessibility of computers and the internet today, the integration of web-technology into the curricula of Korean universities has not found widespread acceptance" (Min, Kim, & Jung, 2000, p. 120).

Alternatively, the Korea National Open University (KNOU) has extensively utilized ICT as a means to deliver instruction. KNOU has also joined with eight traditional universities to form the Korea Virtual University Consortium (KVU), and is collaborating with these universities to design web-based courses. A number of traditional universities also offer credit and non-credit web-based courses, and the 14 college consortium currently forming the Open Cyber University (OCU) operates web-based courses for students of member schools. However, as Eastmond (2000) states, even though

> Asia has more enrolments in open and distance education than anywhere else in the world...Using the United Kingdom's Open University (UKOU) completion rate of 49% as a baseline, completion rates in Asia are much lower: 28% at Indira Gandhi National Open University (OU), 17% at Sukhotai Thammathirat, and only 10% at the Korean National OU (p. 103).

Eastmond (2000) then cautions that attempts to import courses from other nations have failed when transplanted to Asia, due to uniqueness of the local cultural and learning context. Ellis (1994) has also highlighted the problems associated with the transfer of Western teaching styles to Asia, particularly those relating to English language teaching; while Oka (2004), along with Weschler (1997), recently bring into question the applicability and appropriateness of universal English language teaching assumptions and approaches when viewed in relation to the Asian context. Critchley (1998) lends support to this notion by stating that the majority of language learning theories, and theories of language, are developed in contexts where English is taught as a second language, and have largely been transplanted without modification into the EFL context.

Considering such notions, aspects of the cultural learning style and Confucian consciousness of Korean EFL students may hold important implications for the application of computer technology and the design of such systems for effective use with these learners. It is therefore suggested that any design or use of such systems needs to take into account both cultural and learning factors. As O'Hagan (1999) and Warschauer (1996) highlight, CALL effectiveness relies on instructional design methodologies and implementation techniques and does not result from use of the medium itself. This being so, CALL could be made more appropriate to Korean EFL student levels and expectations, and to the local cultural learning context, and address the learning style and 'hidden assumptions' associated with the Confucian consciousness. CALL initiatives in the Korean educational landscape could then, and as Ahn (2002) and I. O. Kim (2000) predict, be more directed to assist in transitioning students from roles of dependent and passive learners to more active and autonomous ones.

Applying CALL in the EFL setting of Korea

To date much research on the use of CALL and the application of computer-based learning, within Korean EFL classes, has centred on the use of computer-mediated communication (CMC) as well as the internet for classroom instruction. There has been limited research on the impact of courseware, unless used collaboratively with learners. This focus results from the resurgence of socio-constructivist views of learning where students are expected to become active constructors of knowledge. Emphasis is placed on computer supported collaborative learning (CSCL) within class time, from the application of network based learning activities to the use of computer-based tools, to support collaborative learning tasks (see Sherry, 1996; Smith, 2001; Spore, 2001).

Computer-mediated communication

CMC is ideal for promoting language learning as it allows for global interaction, but there is realization of the need for pedagogical assessment of the effectiveness of CMC within Korea (D. J. Kim, 2002). However, Min and Choi (2002) find, for EFL students at the elementary school level, that CMC is able to stimulate motivation and language proficiency while allowing for positive variations of language use. CMC has also been put to use by implementing e-mail exchange projects at the university level to develop language skills (Son & O'Neill, 1999) and chat for language skill development at the secondary school level (Cheon,

2003), while Huh (2000) illustrates the use of key-pals in the high school environment to develop speaking, reading, and writing skills.

Recognizing the predominant application of CMC for asynchronous textual communication in Korea, S. Y. Kim (2002a) conducted a study on the use of an avatar-based voice-communication program. This study reveals several distinctions between student perceptions of oral interaction in face-to-face communication (FFC) versus CMC modes. Namely, immediate feedback was more easily achieved through FFC, while use of avatar-based voice CMC saw students report reduction in anxiety and inhibition levels along with increased motivation and interest. In this regard, oral-based CMC is a useful addition to classes, but not a replacement for FFC, as FFC and CMC combined was no better than FFC or CMC alone (S. Y. Kim, 2002b).

E-mail exchange projects have also been initiated to develop the Korean language skills of Australian students and English language skills of Korean students simultaneously. Son and O'Neill (1999) point out that such "task-based cross-cultural communication has the potential to improve students' language skills and cultural awareness" (p. 71), but that clear objectives for communication must be established so that communication between participants does not breakdown.

Although findings of recent research on CMC (refer to Shen, 1999; Becker, 2000; Stepp-Greany, 2002) show promising results for improving writing skills and reducing student language use anxiety, when employing CALL-based tasks such as CMC it is again important to consider the local cultural learning style and educational environment. This employment also needs to take into account the simultaneous implementation of effective learning approaches for the needs of the local EFL learner (e.g., the Korean preference for visual learning). Cheon (2003) illustrates, task-based CMC provides Korean secondary school learners with the opportunity to engage in meaningful negotiation, with pictures playing a significant role in promoting this negotiation, although the effectiveness of CMC for developing the grammatical competence of Korean EFL learners is still uncertain.

The Internet and World Wide Web

The Internet and World Wide Web are useful for CALL purposes as they offer a wide variety of adaptable resources, and provide access for EFL learners to 'authentic' linguistic and cultural content. At the grade school level Shin (2004) highlights several useful web-based resources available to Korean students and teachers, including those relating to developing self-directed learning and listening skills as well as internet-based activities for use in class. The provision of such material as this, by teachers, also provides students with opportunities to further study lesson content outside the classroom in their own time. Another approach, taken in junior high school, is that of developing an internet resource page for grammar instruction, based on the National Curriculum and textbooks (K. C. Jeong, 2002).

Interestingly, while Lee and Kastner (1999) view EFL classes as performance-based, where students select and write summaries of internet resources and then present these orally, they see such activities as

> very challenging for most [Korean] students because they perceive themselves as dependent language learners and expect to be told what to do and how to do it. Being faced with the responsibility and challenge of having to find, summarize, and present materials in this manner at first totally confuses and discombobulates students (p. 29).

Ahn (2002), alternatively, states that Korean teachers traditionally provide teacher-centred classrooms, but through internet use teachers can adjust learners to student-centred teaching through moderate exposure. Further I. O. Kim (2000), introducing the notion of cultural learning styles, stresses that Korean students are accustomed to rote learning, but suggests use of the internet and multimedia-based CALL materials as able to accommodate various learning styles simultaneously.

A Foreign Language Education Centre homepage project is one example, as Lee and Yang (2002) note. Yet, in this context, students regard internet-based listening as having pitfalls, and were ambivalent to the possibility of chat leading to speaking skill improvement. In contrast, most students view internet-based reading tasks as leading to learning gains, as well as writing tasks with e-mail perceived as benefiting language skills. Lee and Pyo (2002), on the other hand, report development of a program to study the effectiveness of both on-/off-line delivery of instruction within a mandatory university EFL course. However, in this initiative, they found offline students were able to consistently outperform online counterparts. Lee and Yang indicate this result is from the student's lack of minimum levels of functional English and learner independence. This also highlights the importance of teacher training to redress these deficiencies, and the need to establish a meaningful learning environment when employing internet and multimedia-based CALL in the EFL context of Korea.

Software and courseware

Educators also have access to a vast number of EFL software packages as well as programs for multimedia creation and editing, and in this regard remastering of material, like the use of CMC or the internet and World Wide Web, has been utilized to reduce the burden of administering English language grade school classes entirely in the target language. In addition, when utilizing multimedia courseware collaboratively with children, it was found that interaction features believed to foster language learning were 25% higher (Y. S. Jung, 2000), and significant differences in listening comprehension and attitude also occurred when friend and non-friend groups were formed. However, the type of group formation did not appear to hold any significant differences relating to oral proficiency development and vocabulary learning. It was also found that CD-ROM titles applied within the Korean EFL university classroom show that students utilizing such material, as well as those conducting only self-study, were able to outperform others (Keem, 2000).

In addition, C. H. Lee (2000) stresses the use of information gaps, but primarily simulations, as a means of providing EFL learners with language practice, and refers to programs such as Storyboard as the means to create such material. Attention is also drawn to the fact that, although such material allows learners to gain control over the learning environment, teachers need to remind Korean students to participate actively in the educational process, as Korean students are passive when directing their language learning (see Lee & Kastner, 1999; Y. J. Lee, 2000; Jung, 2002). Y. S. Jung (2000) remarks, "Only when students got some instructions on what to do or how to do it, they did as instructed" (p. 43).

Confucian consciousness and CALL in Korea

CALL initiatives in the Korean educational environment, overviewed above, have been employed to greater or lesser extent and with varying degrees of success. Yet, one important aspect appears to have been consistently under emphasized. That is, the impact of the local cultural context and learning environment, both on the development of CALL material for use with learners as well as on the means by which such material should be employed. This is a particularly critical notion to examine as cultural contexts, and coping with cultural differences in the learning process of students, and the impact of this on teaching and learning styles is significant.

By being sensitive to the Korean educational environment, one may sense future opportunities for all types of CALL use in Korea that are appropriately attuned to the local cultural context. Some insights into this teaching and learning context are highlighted, as Soper (1997) notes, students objecting to the development of their own learning, and believing "a teacher should dictate knowledge to them" (p.18), came from teaching backgrounds of a traditional nature; and, Korean students, as Min, et al. (2000) illustrate, strongly agree with the attitude that the teacher is responsible for the learning of students. Importantly, these factors hold implications for the implementation of CALL within Confucian-based societies like Korea. As Hofstede (cited in Joo, 1997) states, the Confucian mind-set sees the role of the teacher as 'an authoritative figure', where "effectiveness of learning is related to the excellence of the teacher", and so "students expect teachers to have [and provide] all of the answers" (Learning Styles, para. 2). So too, Eastmond (2000) notes that "in many Asian countries the teacher is a 'sensei' or guru figure who imparts knowledge and wisdom, and the role of the student is to listen carefully, learn deeply, and apply that wisdom" (p. 104). Within Korea, Park and Oxford (1988) further illustrate that language learning is perceived by students as teacher-centred, and "most EFL teachers in Korea remain the primary source of action and linguistic input—the main 'actors' in the classroom" (p. 107).

This 'teacher as expert' paradigm, relies on transfer rather than creation of knowledge, and sees students regarding themselves as dependent learners engaging in individualistic memorization and rote learning rather than participants in the collectivist creation of knowledge leading to learning. Yet, even though Rhee, Uleman, and Lee (in Windle, 2003) remind us that the "individualism-collectivism construct is not so straightforward" (p. 7), Confucian tradition still encourages master/apprentice relationships and a culture of learning that "promotes teacher dependency for passive students, a tradition hard to reverse" (Eastmond, 2000, p. 104). As such, in Korea, the 'empty-vessel' argument of teaching and learning has been, and still is, predominant, and "in many respects English-teaching and language learning methods in Korea have not yet caught up with the times. Centuries-old methods of dealing with both teaching and learning languages are still closely adhered to" (Shaffer, 2001, p. 1).

The Confucian consciousness

Antecedent research shows that "each culture has its own distinctive value systems and orientations which illuminate what is of significance within that society" (Kluckhohn & Strodtbeck cited in Hyun, 2001, p. 205). In Korea today, Confucianism thrives more than in any other Asian nation including China and Japan (Crowder Han, 1995), and pervades everyday Korean life (Hyun, 2001). Breen (1999) also notes that Koreans have adopted "…Chinese Confucianism in a more extreme application than the Chinese themselves" (p. 12) and have outdone their elder brother "China, in its application of Confucianism" (p. 43). These precepts generate a cultural learning style that strongly influences means of acquiring knowledge, and as Joyce and Weil (1986) highlight, a people's culture strongly influences their personalities and ways of communication. Although it is also vital to realize that an individual's values can vary greatly within a culture (Hyun, 2001), and it is essential to see people both as individuals and members of a cultural group (Kalaboukas cited in Armitage, 2001). Nonetheless, the cultural notions Korean EFL students maintain do affect their classroom behaviour, educational development, and use of English language skills, as well as guide their interaction with native-speakers. It is the perspective of this chapter that such behaviour also impacts upon the use of CALL, both in self-access and collaborative modes, and results from the means by which students expect to acquire knowledge, and as such needs to be considered in the design and application of such material. Taking the local cultural and learning context into account may then allow even greater promise for the effectiveness of CALL initiatives in Korea. Accordingly, further explanation of the cultural background, and Confucian mindset, is warranted.

The Confucian consciousness, as documented by Cortazzi (1990), is responsible for many of the 'hidden assumptions' concerning teaching methods, lesson content, and learner expectations that students like Koreans exhibit within classrooms. Hyun (2001) also refers to Hofstede (1986), as does Joo (1997), who focuses on cultural differences in learner/teacher interactions throughout the world. Hofstede, reporting on the Confucian consciousness, sees problematic situations between teacher and student arising from differences in social position; differing student perceptions of curriculum relevance between two societies; profiles of cognitive abilities; and, expected patterns of interaction. In spite of this, although much research linking the Confucian consciousness and Korean classroom interactions has been undertaken (refer to Gray, 1998; Robertson, 2002a, 2002b, 2003; Shaffer, 2001; Lim & Griffith, 2003; Windle, 2003), with the impact of the Confucian consciousness on elements such as discussions within the EFL classroom (in Cronin, 1995; Lim & Griffith, 2003) and teacher-student interaction (see Breen, 1999; Min, et al., 2000) well-recognized, there is still limited literature detailing specifically how such notions of interaction in the Korean

EFL classroom come to affect the use of media and computer systems for learning. Although Y. J. Lee (2000) does indicate that, rather than being forums of communication and discussion, English Educational TV programs tend to be language lessons, and such programs "are merely promoting the Korean identity as in the dependent second language [learner] mode", and laments "the content and presentation clearly portray the audience as helpless and dependent learners" (pp. 107-108).

The Korean cultural learning style

"Though some Korean students may express complete disinterest in Confucianism, they still remain bound by its approach to disciplinary habits of work and study, life and play" (Korean Overseas Information Service cited in Cronin, 1995, para. 9). Cronin, from her teaching of Korean students, discovered that learners would respond to certain class activities with statements like 'the professor is the expert; we have never before been given a choice'. Breen (1999) also states that questioning, even at university, is viewed as an insult and challenge to the teacher. This kind of student outlook also impacts upon the native English speaking instructor, culturally used to dealing with university students on more of an equal level and used to facilitating an environment from which students can create knowledge.

A teacher-student interaction study by Armitage (2001), and another by Choi (cited in Armitage, 2001), examines Korean EFL students living and studying abroad and the difficulties experienced in relationships with lecturers, tutors, and peer students. Further, Lee (in Armitage) highlights the Korean lack of confidence in communicative English in university English classes taught by native-speakers, and determines that such lack of confidence stems from a focus on reading and writing as well as the limited opportunities Korean students have to speak English. Lee also mentions that differences arising from the teacher-student relationship may affect the development of student confidence when speaking in English with native-speakers. Interestingly, the difficulty of speaking, with native-speaker teachers, experienced by Korean students in Korea, as presented by Lee, is mirrored by Choi as the main difficulty Korean students experience when studying abroad. Additionally, as Windle (2003) points out, Korean EFL students perceive classroom environments of native-speakers to be different from that of Koreans, and students tend not to use specific English expressions since Korean equivalents would be impolite. This last point implies the native-language produces an affective cultural barrier over the second language linguistic use of

Korean EFL students, stemming from Confucian consciousness and in this case relating to politeness strategies.

It should also be mentioned that the 'collectivist' nature of Korean society, illustrated by the Hofstede (1986) study, along with group-centeredness presented by Armitage (2001), would not by its very nature be at variance with a collaborative use of multimedia activities and CMC if culturally attuned and adapted to the Korean EFL classroom. Yet, regardless of the group-oriented nature of Koreans, findings from contemporary research show that Korean students have difficulty gaining the full benefit from group activities (Armitage, 2001), and prefer structure and formality to group-based learning (C. C. Park, 2002). Armitage relates these findings to the educational system where students mostly concentrate on memorization over practical skills development. Yet how the impact of such notions affect learning with CALL initiatives, and use of collaborative CMC and network-based group tasks within the EFL classroom, has not been a focus of Korean-based research, and this is perhaps because, as I. O. Kim (2000) states, "collaborative learning is predicated on a culture that values collectivism" (p. 39).

CALL and the Korean cultural learning style

Following a global trend there is strong emphasis today on the use in Korea of collaborative CMC and CALL activities that focus on autonomous learning. However, their use stands in conflict with the dependent learner construct students possess, and strong beliefs that the teacher is ultimately responsible for the learning of a student. In addition, social delegations, such as respect for the teacher and the existence of senior-junior status levels amongst all members of Korean society, sees relationships and responsibilities formed between those of different status, gender, and age, enter the native-speakers EFL classroom whether the native-speaker teacher is culturally blind to them or not.

Yet reduction of teacher-student talk, and an increase in student-student interaction, can see learners engage in interaction with people of relatively equal social power, as well as low social distance, although perceived gender differentials may still enter the equation in this form of classroom interaction, along with the notions of noonchi (reading another's mind, and using tact accordingly), chemyon (social face), and uri ('our', or rather the collectivist 'us'). Similar forms of cultural interaction between students and computers can be achieved, structured to reflect what is believed to be Korean classroom expectations, such as group dependence, allowing students to work towards consensus, and avoid disagreements to obtain social harmony. That is, where student-student interaction is undertaken through collaborative-based CMC and network-based activities. However, elements of intragroup interaction leading to differential performance among students may yet appear, resulting from the cultural bonds that guide their relationships; Kim (2000) reminds us most foreign language students live in monolingual/monocultural environments and are culture-bound, as their entire world view is determined by values gained through a single cultural environment.

In this regard, the self-access approach of computer-based activities may have a place in the Korean EFL cultural learning environment. That is not to say there is a need to revert to the behaviourist use of such materials, or total reliance on them, but such materials, particularly if applied in the homework setting during the learning stage of language acquisition, can allow for the perception of the 'teacher as expert' paradigm to be transferred to computer-based applications. This is one method of employing CALL that takes into account a Confucianist approach, and embodies elements of the Korean cultural learning style. The computer can then fulfil the role of a mentor-based system for students, affording them the direction and guidance they need when learning, and if associated activities are designed appropriately can be extended to allow learners to negotiate meaning from activities, in sociocultural terms, from a Zone of Proximal Development (see Vygotsky, 1978). In this manner students can also become exposed to the nature of autonomous, independent, and interactive learning, and led away from more teacher dependent means of acquiring knowledge.

Independent language learning, in terms of CALL, can also offer a self-contained learning environment in which students can become active rather than passive recipients of information (Klassen, Detaramani, Lui, Patri, & Wu, 1998). This will assist in developing levels of learner independence and functional English skills that Lee and Pyo (2002) indicate students require when undertaking collaborative CMC and CALL activities focusing on autonomous learning, particularly from within the classroom during the practice stages of language acquisition. Use of self-access materials also ensures delivery of the same content to students in mandatory study programs, such as the university English setting, and it is the individual who must ultimately take the most important role in the development of their own language skills in such educational contexts.

In addition, self-access approaches to computer-based activities, while rigorously providing for student needs and purposes, yet allow for autonomous context-based learner-centred and learner-controlled study at a time and pace convenient for the student, and can diminish the cultural bonds of perceived social status and required interactions resulting from these bonds. This, taking one example, includes the cultural factor of saving 'face', and in this regard Song (cited in Min, 1998) refers to saving face as 'perfectionism'. That is, where 'perfectionism' refers to the tendency to save face by not making mistakes in public and avoiding situations which may lead to making such mistakes. It is further envisioned that the outward display of 'perfectionism' by Koreans in public settings such as classrooms would also come into play within group interaction within class time, as well as one-to-one or collaborative CMC, seeing students working to lessen 'fear of failure' by not as actively engaging in learning. However, with a sensitive and culturally attuned approach to the use of CALL, befitting the local educational context, it is suggested that such factors can be alleviated through the use of self-access multimedia programs in the homework learning phase, followed by, or combined with, appropriately applied classroom CMC in the practice phase, in addition to traditional taught course methods and approaches. This would provide students with a zone of comfort in which to make mistakes as they explore learning in an environment where 'fear of failure' can be minimized, and where errors can provide a scaffolding of knowledge that allows students to autonomously and independently learn from their mistakes (see D.Chun, 1994; Erstad, 1996; Malhotra, 2002), and then, in turn, afford them with the opportunity to actively apply this knowledge in practice.

Conclusion

Sweeping educational reforms concerning English language education and ICT use within classes in Korea are now beginning to filter from policy into practice. Nevertheless, the tertiary sector lacks alignment with e-learning initiatives established by the government for the grade school sector. This process has been hampered by emphasizing ICT use for administrative purposes and research rather than development of effective e-learning strategies. As a result computer-based education within mandatory university English programs, as well as native-speaker classes, is virtually non-existent. However, individual Korean educators at all levels of the education chain are incorporating CALL to a greater or lesser extent within their EFL classrooms. CALL use in this regard largely focuses on computer-supported collaborative learning, and perhaps is partly due to the compulsory use of computer assisted instruction for 10% of grade school class time. Likewise, global trends outside of Korea are focusing on the resurgence of socio-constructivist views of learning which is in turn changing the Korean approach to CALL implementation. Furthermore, universities have begun to mandate required achievement levels on standardized English language tests as well as proficiency in computer literacy as graduation requirements. All of these factors therefore result in the establishment of both ICT and improved English language usage. These far-reaching modifications are recognized by Korean students and educators and will continue into the 21st century.

Despite this recognition, it is suggested that the Confucian consciousness, which so deeply penetrates Korean society in terms of education and the generation of a cultural learning style, continues to strongly impact the means of acquiring knowledge. Consequently, this consciousness may affect how students approach education when utilizing media and computer-based systems in both collaborative and self-access modes. It is therefore important to recognize the impact of this intellectual paradigm and keep it in mind to guide design principles behind the generation of learning content for these students, as well as any application of CALL initiatives with them. Particularly since, as I. S. Lee (2002) reminds us, cyberspace is a highly learner-centred and self-regulated learning environment, where learners must take responsibility for what and how to learn. Such learner autonomy is a central issue for the success of most computer-based initiatives, and empowering students as learners is the essence of 'autonomy' according to Holec (in Benson and Voller, 1997). Therefore, future studies relating to CALL in Korea should focus on the interplay of the local cultural and learning context, rather than pushing it aside as most to date have tended to do, and centre on the actual processes students employ to acquire knowledge from such material. CALL initiatives in the Korean educational landscape could then serve to assist in transitioning students from roles of somewhat dependent and passive learners to more active, autonomous, and perhaps even more analytical ones, well-suited to the independent creation of knowledge through the use of multimedia, self-access approaches, CMC, and collaborative CALL. Findings from such future studies would then assist in developing methods and models of multimedia comprehension, grounded in the local cultural and learning context, from which CALL could be developed and applied to most effectively assist the Korean learner with English language acquisition.

References

Ahn, B. (2002). An instructional model for college English incorporating the World Wide Web. *Journal of the Applied Linguistics Association of Korea, 18*(1), 195-218.

Armitage, L. (2001). *Factors affecting the adjustment of Koreans studying in Australia.* Australia-Korea Foundation. Retrieved February 4, 2003, from http://www.dfat.gov.au/akf/laa_images/laa_contents.html

Becker, H. (2000). *Pedagogical motivation for student computer use that lead to student engagement.* Retrieved January 27, 2003, from http://www.crito.uci.edu/tlc/findings/spec_rpt_pedegogical/ped_mot_pdf.pdf

Benson, P., & Voller, P. (1997). Autonomy and independence in language learning. London: Longman.

Breen, M. (1999). *The Koreans.* Great Britain: Orion Business.

Cheon, H. (2003). The viability of computer mediated communication in the Korean secondary EFL classroom. *Asian EFL Journal,* March 2003. Retrieved March 16, 2004, from: http://www.asian-efl-journal.com/march03.sub2.htm

Choi, S. Y., Kim, K. S., Lee, C. K., & Sol, Y. H. (1999). Effective use of multimedia computer courseware in English language teaching and learning. *Multimedia Assisted Language Learning, 2*(1), 179-256.

Chun, D. (1994). Using computer networking to facilitate the acquisition of interactive competence. *System, 2*(1), 17-31.

Chun, H. (2002). The CD-ROM review and evaluation guidelines for listening and speaking in the high school English textbook of Korean 7th curriculum. *A new paradigm for innovative multimedia language education in the 21st century* (pp.353-363). Proceedings of the Korean Association of Multimedia Assisted Language Learning, October 3-5, 2002. Seoul: Korea.

Critchley, M. (1998). *Design and Implementation of a communicative approach for entry-level university students.* Josai International University Kiyou.

Cortazzi, M. (1990). Cultural and educational expectations in the language classroom. In B. Harrison (Ed.), *Culture and the language classroom* (pp. 54-65). London: Macmillan Press.

Cronin, M. (1995). Considering the cultural context in teaching and learning for Korean tertiary students by western teachers. In Summers, L. (Ed.), *A focus on learning* (pp. 53-56). Proceedings of the 4th Annual Teaching and

Learning Forum, Edith Cowan University, February 1995. Perth: Edith Cowan University. Retrieved July 9, 2003, from http://lsn.curtin.edu.au/tlf/tlf1995/cronin.html

Crowder Han, S. (1995). *Notes on things Korean.* Seoul: Hollym Corporation.

Cuban, L. (2001). *Oversold and underused: Computers in the classroom.* Cambridge: Harvard University Press.

Eastmond, D. (2000). Realizing the promise of distance education in low technology countries. *Educational Technology, Research, and Development, 48*(2), 100-125.

Elgort, I., Marshall, S., & Mitchell, G. (2003). *NESB student perceptions and attitudes to a new online learning environment.* The Higher Education Research and Development Society of Australasia Conference, July 6-9 2003. Christchurch: New Zealand. Retrieved July 26, 2003, from: http://surveys.canterbury.ac.nz/herdsa03/pdfsref/Y1049.pdf

Ellis, G. (1994). Contributions of cross-cultural research in the transfer of western teaching styles to Vietnam. *Asia-Pacific Exchange Journal, 1*(1).

Erstad, O. (1996). *Multimedia in educational settings: Prospects for learning. Manuscript series on communication: technology and culture.* Retrieved March 16, 2004, from: http://www.intermedia.uio.no/ktk/notater/pdf/notat4.pdf

Gray, R. (1998). Confucian conundrums: Higher education and ESL teaching in Korea and Japan. *Advancing our profession: Perspectives on teacher development and education.* Proceedings of the 1998 Korea TESOL Conference, October 16-18. Seoul: Korea. Retrieved July 26, 2003, from: http://www.kotesol.org/pubs/proceedings/1998/gray.pdf

Hofstede, G. (1986). Cultural differences in teaching and learning. *International Journal of Intercultural Relations, 10,* 301-320.

Huh, J. (2000). A study of English teaching and learning using the internet: the case of key-pal activities. *Multimedia Assisted Language Learning, 3*(1), 287-308.

Hyun, K. (2001). Sociocultural change and traditional values: Confucian values among Koreans and Korean Americans. *International Journal of Intercultural Relations, 25*, 203-229.

Jeon, J., & Kim, E. (2001). Teacher training through self-observation. *Journal of the Applied Linguistics Association of Korea, 17*(2), 157-177.

Jeong, K. C. (2002). Web-based language learning: A case study. *A new paradigm for innovative multimedia language education in the 21st century* (pp. 254-261). Proceedings of the Korean Association of Multimedia Assisted Language Learning, October 3-5, 2002. Seoul: Korea.

Joo, Y. (1997). Teaching the grammar of narratives to Korean EFL students. *Journal of English Grammar on the Web,* 1. Retrieved April 24, 2001, from http://www.gsu.edu/~wwwesl/issue1/joo.htm

Joyce, B., & Weil, M. (1986). *Models of teaching* (3rd Ed.). Sydney: Allyn and Bacon.

Jung, I. (2000). Korea's experiments with virtual education. *Education and Technology Notes Series, 5*(2). World Bank Human Development Network.

Jung, Y. S. (2000). Effects of a cooperative learning approach to MALL (Multimedia Assisted Language Learning). *Multimedia Assisted Language Learning, 3*(1), 9-46.

Keem, S. U. (2000). A field study: multimedia assisted English instruction to cultivate communicative competence. *Multimedia Assisted Language Learning, 3*(1), 139-166.

KERIS. (2001). *Adapting education to the information age: A white paper.* Ministry of Education and Human Resources Development, Korean Education and Research Information Service. Retrieved January 27, 2003, from http://www.keris.or.kr/english/2001-WhitePap.pdf

Kim, D. J. (2002). A study on the pedagogical models for the optimum efficacy of CMC instruction. *Multimedia Assisted Language Learning, 5*(2), 46-74.

Kim, I. O. (2000). Accommodating language learners' different learning styles with multimedia technology. *Multimedia Assisted Language Learning, 3*(2), 36-52.

Kim, S. A. (2000). Enhancing cultural understanding: An instructional model. *English Teaching, 55*(4), 141-166.

Kim, S. Y. (2002a). Teachers' perceptions about teaching English through English. *English Teaching, 57*(1), 131-148.

Kim, S. Y. (2002b). The marriage of CMC and FFC: Its effects on Korean students' oral proficiency in English. *A new paradigm for innovative multimedia language education in the 21st century* (pp. 326-334). Proceedings of the Korean Association of Multimedia Assisted Language Learning, October 3-5, 2002. Seoul: Korea.

Klassen, J., Detaramani, C., Lui, E., Patri, M., & Wu, J. (1998). Does self-access learning at the tertiary level really work? *Asian Journal of English Language Teaching, 8*, 55-80.

Kwon, O. Y. (2000). Korea's English education policy changes in the 1990s: Innovations to gear the nation for the 21st century. *English Teaching, 55*(1), 47-91.

Lee, C. H. (2000). Communicative activities applicable to CALL: Based on computer simulations. *Multimedia Assisted Language Learning, 3*(2), 70-99.

Lee, C. H., & Pyo, K. H. (2002). The development and implementation of the online/offline English language education program (OELEP). *A new paradigm for innovative multimedia language education in the 21st century* (pp. 69-80). Proceedings of the Korean Association of Multimedia Assisted Language Learning, October 3-5, 2002. Seoul: Korea.

Lee, C. I., & Yang, E. M. (2002). Integrating CALL into classroom practices: Its theory and application. *A new paradigm for innovative multimedia language education in the 21st century* (pp. 169-183). Proceedings of the Korean Association of Multimedia Assisted Language Learning, October 3-5, 2002. Seoul: Korea.

Lee, H. (2001). The role of native-English-speaking teachers in the Korean EFL education system. *The Internet TEFL Journal, 32*. Retrieved February 7, 2003, from http://www.mantoman.co.kr/issues/m032/m3201.htm

Lee, I. S. (2002). Gender differences in self-regulated on-line learning strategies within Korea's university context. *Educational Technology, Research, and Design, 50*(1), 101-121.

Lee, M. (2001). A critical analysis of mandatory computer education for elementary school children in Korea: In the aspect of intellectual development. *Enhancement of quality learning through information and communication technology*. Proceedings of the International Conference on Computers in Education, 2001. Seoul, Korea. Retrieved August, 23, 2002, from http://www.icce2001.org/cd/pdf/p11/kr047.pdf

Lee, Y. J., & Kastner, M. (1999). Multimedia in performance-based EFL classes. *Multimedia Assisted Language Learning, 2*(1), 21-34.

Li, D. (1998). It's always more difficult than you plan and imagine: Teachers' perceived difficulties in introducing the communicative approach in South Korea. *TESOL Quarterly, 32*(4), 677-703.

Lim, H. Y., & Griffith, W. I. (2003). Successful classroom discussions with adult Korean ESL/EFL learners. *The Internet TESL Journal, IX*(5). Retrieved May 18, 2003 from http://iteslj.org/Techniques/Lim-AdultKoreanshtml

Malhotra, B. (2002). *Shut the classroom doors! The computers must stay! Or reintegrating reading and writing skills through computer-mediated-communication*. Curriculum, Testing, and new technologies: The way ahead. Second National ELT Conference, March 27-28. Muscat, Oman. Retrieved March 16, 2004, from:
http://www.omc.edu.om/bina/Shut_the_Classroom_door_paper.htm

Min, B. (1998). A study of the attitudes of Korean adults toward technology-assisted language learning. *Multimedia-Assisted Language Learning, 1*(1), 63-78.

Min, D., & Choi, E. I. (2002). Using CMC to improve elementary school students' English proficiency: Focused on the analysis of discourse functions and syntactic complexity. *Multimedia Assisted Language Learning, 5*(2), 103-129.

Min, S. J., Kim, H. K., and Jung, K. T. (2000). A paradigm shift in English education in Korea: Integration of the textbook to a Web-based curriculum. *Multimedia Assisted Language Learning, 3*(1), 119-138.

O'Hagan, C. (1999). Embedding ubiquitous educational technology: Is it possible, do we want it, and, if so, how do we achieve it? *Educational Technology and Society, 2*(4), 19-22.

Oka, H. (2004). A non-native approach to ELT: Universal or Asian? *Asian EFL Journal*, March 2004. Retrieved March, 16, 2004 from: http://www.asian-efl-journal.com/04_ho.pdf

Park, C. C. (2002). Crosscultural differences in learning styles of secondary English learners. *Bilingual Research Journal, 26*(2), 443-459.

Park, J. Y. (2002). *Amendments for the College Entrance Exam System for 2005 School Year*. Ministry of Education and Human Resources Development. Retrieved February 4, 2003, from http://content.moe.go.kr/eng/engmoebbs/Entrance_Exam_System.doc

Park, S. O. (1998). Globalization in Korea: Dream and reality. *GeoJournal, 45*(1), 123-128.

Park, Y., & Oxford, R. (1998). Changing roles for teachers in the English village course in Korea. *System, 26*, 107-113.

Robertson, P. (2002a). Asian EFL Research Protocols. *Asian EFL Journal*, December 2002. Retrieved March, 16, 2004 from: http://asian-efl-journal.com/decart2002a.htm

Robertson, P. (2002b). The pervading influence of neo-Confucianism on the Korean education system. *Asian EFL Journal*, June 2002. Retrieved March, 16, 2004 from: http://asian-efl-journal.com/june2002.conf.htm

Robertson, P. (2003). Teaching English pronunciation skills to the Asian learner: A cultural complexity or subsumed piece of cake? *Asian EFL Journal*, June 2003. Retrieved March, 16, 2004 from: http://www.asian-efl-journal.com/june2003subpr.htm

Shaffer, D. (2001). A new approach for a new language. *The Internet TEFL Journal, 35*. Retrieved July 26, 2003 from: http://www.mantoman.co.kr/issues/m035/m3510.htm

Shen, J. (1999). Learner anxiety and computer-assisted writing. *CALL-EJ Online, 3*(2). Retrieved January 27. 2003, from http://www.lerc.ritsumei.ac.jp/callej/3-2/shen.html

Sherry, L. (1996). Issues in distance learning. *International Journal of Educational Telecommunications, 1*(4), 337-365.

Shin, M. N. (2004). Learning with the Web resources. The Internet TEFL Journal, 48. Retrieved July 26, 2003 from http://www.mantoman.co.kr/study/stu_02.php?wz_indx=48&indx=4&num=382

Smith, J. (2001). Modeling the social construction of knowledge in ELT teacher education. *ELT Journal, 55*(3), 221-227.

Son, J.-B. & O'Neill, S. (1999). Collaborative e-mail exchange: A pilot study of peer editing. *Multimedia Assisted Language Learning, 2*(2), 69-87.

Soper, J. (1997). Integrating interactive media in courses: The WinEcon software with workbook approach. *Journal of Interactive Media in Education, 97*(2), 1-39. Retrieved January 27, 2003, from http://www-jime.open.ac.uk/97/2/winecon-01.html

Spore, M. A. (2001). *Wired writing: A review of issues and possibilities of electronic writing centres.* Saskatoon, Canada: University of Saskatchewan, Instructional Design Extension Division. Retrieved March 16, 2004, from http://www.extension.usask.ca/ExtensionDivision/about/Staff/q-t/pdf/wiredwriting.pdf

Stepp-Greany, J. (2002). Student perception on language learning in a technological environment: Implications for the new millennium. *Language Learning & Technology, 6*(1), 165-180.

UNESCO. (2002). ICT policies of selected countries in the Asia-Pacific: South Korea. *ICT for Education in Asia-Pacific.* United Nations Educational, Scientific and Cultural Organization.

Vygotsky, L. S. (1978). *Mind in society: The development of higher psychological process.* (Cole, M. V., V. John-Steiner, S. Scribner, & E. Souberman, Eds. and Trans.). Cambridge: Harvard University Press.

Warschauer, M. (1996). Computer-assisted language learning: An introduction. In Fotos S. (Ed.), *Multimedia language teaching* (pp. 3-20). Tokyo: Logos International.

Weschler, R. (1997). Uses of Japanese (L1) in the English classroom: Introducing the functional-translation method. *The internet TESL journal, III*(11). Retrieved July 23, 2003 from:
http://iteslj.org/Articles/Weschler-UsingL1.html

Windle, S. (2003). Culture in the Korean EFL classroom: A humanizing process. *The English Connection, 7*(1). KOTESOL Newsletter.

5

Language teacher trainees as multimedia designers: Voices from a CALL classroom

Arif Altun

Abstract

The notion of using computers as a language learning and teaching tool is being diverted to the question of how to design more interactive language learning environments for language learners. This study looks at English as second/foreign language (ESL/EFL) teacher trainees' meaning construction processes while working on designing their own multimedia applications. Seven teams of teacher trainees (n= 27), were asked to design their own multimedia pieces in a project. It was found that teacher trainees perceived multimedia design process as a valuable experience to be transferred into their future teaching careers. In addition, four categories of multimedia design roles were suggested: Media Fans, Navigation Builders, Content Developers, and Fun Seekers. These roles have been shaped through their social interactions in a learning environment.

Introduction

The notion of using computers as a language learning and teaching tool is being diverted to the question of how to design more interactive language learning environments for language learners. Computer assisted language learning (CALL) developers are also being urged to focus on engaging learners in second language (L2) tasks to maximize opportunities for interaction (Pica, Kanagy & Falodun, 1993). Such initiatives would inquire the usefulness of viewing multimedia and multimedia design from the perspective of the input it can provide to learners, the output it allows them to produce, and the interactions they are able to engage in (Chappelle, 1998; Warshauer & Healey, 1998).

Language teachers are being expected to be active CALL users, have the purposes of using CALL (e.g., Son, 2002), and integrate computer technologies into their teaching (Egbert, Paulus & Nakamichi, 2002). Yet, such integration is not unproblematic. Firstly, it is important to equip teacher trainees with the appropriate skills in using technology, and to provide them experience with CALL tools during their pre-service education. Secondly, teachers' first hand experiences, especially their implementations of computer applications, are important indicators to transform classroom environments into technology enhanced learning environments. As Hutchings et al. (1992) put it: "those who prepare the course material may learn much more than those who receive it" (p. 172). Hence, providing teachers first-hand experiences provides a support for life long learning to be extended throughout their professional careers.

For these purposes, an elective CALL course has been designed and implemented in a project-based approach throughout a 16-week long semester in a language teacher education program. This case study describes the development stages of a CALL course and reports on (a) the teacher trainees' perceptions about the usefulness of multimedia design from their own experiences, and (b) their socio-cognitive roles as emerging instructional designers in tasks that required them to transform their language and computer skills into a multimedia piece.

The reviewed literature below includes two separate but interrelated foci: Design as a constructive meaning making process and project-based approach in CALL. Together, these complementary foci present a picture of understanding the design process and the role of projects in the implementation of CALL in authentic context with teacher trainees.

Design as a constructive meaning making process

Recent paradigmatic changes in the field of language learning shifted the instructional practices from the transmissive activities (i.e., drilling, testing, and repetitious) to more active, negotiable, participative (e.g., Pica, 1994), and socially mediated forms of instructional activities. Moreover, active use of language learning has been challenged by the idea of active negotiation and interactions with peers, engagement in process oriented tasks in constructivist environments, and ultimately, overall competence in use and understanding of the target language (Larsen-Freeman & Long, 1991; Ellis, 1999).

In this study, the constructivist model of learning was used. According to constructivists, learning is the process of constructing knowledge from experiences (Driscoll, 1984); social constructivists believe that full cognitive development is accumulated by learners through social interactions (Vygotsky, 1978). With the introduction of multimedia technologies to learning environments, learners engage in the experience of interacting with various media forms which represent knowledge. In addition, by learning to design their own learning environments, they have the opportunities to represent their messages with the help of various media. Therefore, the process of knowledge construction relies not only on the individual learner but also on the interactive environment.

Recently, second language educators have been leaning towards the notion of increasing the degree of autonomy which learners exercise over their learning (Wenden, 1991). In addition, having learners engaged in designing multimedia applications provide them with rich learning experiences and locus of control (Beatty, 2003). Beatty (2003) defines locus of control as the continuum between the learner's responsibility for decisions about the outcomes, sequence of learning, learner interactions and the content. Jonassen, Wilson, Wang and Grabinger (1993) point out the two ends of the continuum as representing objectivist and constructivist orientations toward learning. Multimedia authoring stands on the constructivist end of the continuum where learners develop their language as a long-term activity juxtaposing with making and representing their own meaning.

The function of designing multimedia in a CALL class provides students with a constructivist environment situated within a larger cultural context, that of interactive media (Kafai, Carter-Ching & Marshall, 1997). Working with multiple and interactive media requires a collaborative effort from each participating member. According to Altun (2003), such collaborative effort is essential for social interaction during meaning construction process. Hence, having students engaged with creating their own multimedia application appears to be a meaningful context for them to learn about group work, negotiation, and learning from each other in a collaborative task. Consequently, the product will be the representations of their own meaning construction process.

Design process and project-based approach

CALL course has been designed to provide teacher trainees first hand experiences in developing, that is authoring, their own multimedia teaching materials to be used in real-life settings. Since project-based learning functions as a bridge between using English in class and using English in real life situations outside of class (Fried-Booth, 1997), it places learners in situations where they can use authentic language in groups (either in pair or teams). When working in their groups, they need to develop and apply skills in planning, organizing, negotiating, and arriving at a conclusion upon given tasks. Working on projects in groups also enables individuals to realize their own strengths and preferred ways of learning (e.g., by reading, writing, listening, or speaking) as well as strengthen the work of the team as a whole (Lawrence, 1997).

According to Wrigley (1998), the basic phases found in most projects include selecting a topic, making plans, researching, developing products, and sharing results with others. Van Duzer and Moss (1998) assert the following principles which characterize Project-based learning:

- Builds on previous work;

- Integrates speaking, listening, reading, and writing skills;

- Incorporates collaborative team work, problem solving, negotiating and other interpersonal skills;

- Requires learners to engage in independent work;

- Challenges learners to use English in new and different contexts outside the class;

- Involves learners in choosing the focus of the project and in the planning process;

- Engages learners in acquiring new information that is important to them;

- Leads to clear outcomes; and

- Incorporates self-evaluation, peer evaluation, and teacher evaluation.

Since these principles are in harmony with a constructivist view of learning, and they offer great potential for student-centered, and collaborative approaches to learning (Nunan, 1999), the project-based approach was undertaken to understand the process of EFL language teacher trainees' meaning construction processes during a multimedia design task. More specifically, this study was designed to explore (a) how ESL/EFL teacher trainees' perceive the usefulness of multimedia design; and (b) what are their socio-cognitive roles as emerging instructional designers in a cooperative project.

Methodology

Research context and participants

This study took place in an undergraduate English language teacher-training program in a university setting. A class of 27 junior level teacher trainees, twenty females and seven males, volunteered to participate in this study. All the participants had taken a basic introductory course on the use of computers a year ago. During their course in the previous year, they were taught how to use word processing, spreadsheets, and presentation software packages.

The participating students were enrolled in a semester long elective CALL course for the fall 2001. None of them had any programming or designing experience before the start of the course. The course blended an understanding of the historical development of CALL, CALL methodology, and integrative CALL. The class met every week for 150 min. for a total of 14 weeks. The first five weeks focused mostly on learning about CALL and basics of multimedia design. The course syllabus and task descriptions were posted on the course website, developed by the researcher (for the course syllabus, see, http://cc.ibu.edu.tr/aaltun/courses/CALL/).

Another purpose of this course was to enable students to get in-depth, hands-on experience with a variety of graphics, sound, and text to design and produce their own multimedia. The last nine weeks, therefore, were devoted to authoring and using various software tools to enable them to develop their own graphics, texts, sound and animations for their project-based tasks.

The instructor gave lectures on the multimedia design process and provided direct instruction on how to use these tools. Students worked through these software packages to prepare their materials for their final products. They were also introduced a couple of CD-ROM titles to evaluate as in-class activities.

At the very beginning of the semester, students were asked to form groups to study through projects. Students were given flexibility to form their own groups; no intervention was made by the instructor. In the second week of the semester, they formed a total of seven groups, ranging from two to five members in each group. The groups were asked to plan, organize, design, develop and present their own open-ended multimedia product as an outcome of their learning process. The group names and the participants in each group are as follows: S'CALL'ERS (Fatih, Sema, Serdar), The BEATLES (Nihal, Hacer), GROUP TECH (Ercan, Oncel, Ugur, Tolga, Zeynep), DIGITAL SUCCESS (Selver, Hacer, Hale, Aynur, Aysegul), GROUP MOUSE (Yurdagul, Nuray, Nilgun, Havacan,

Habibe), GROUP MONITOR (Erdogan, Burcu, Ozlem), FISH 'N' CHIPS (Gulin, Eda, Anıl, Emel).

The general format of the course was partly a mixture of demonstration, discussion, and lecturing; but, largely a hands-on experience of designing multimedia. These hours were carried out in the computer lab. The computer lab consisted of 16 stand-alone computers. These were Pentium II 333 MhZ with 32 MB Ram and 3.2 GB HDD PCs. Only 10 of them had sound cards available. Two microphones and 4 speakers were available in the lab. None of the computers had neither an Internet connection, nor a CD-R or any kind of external media storage device attached. They were running Windows 98 operating system, with no antivirus protection software installed. All computers had a ghost image available so that the whole system could be reinstalled in less than 10 minutes if the systems crashed.

Tasks for this course

During this course, students were asked to do weekly readings, engage in discussions, and design a multimedia product. Students were introduced to the notion of authoring. They were instructed to develop a project at the end of the semester. As an authoring suite, an authoring tool HyperStudio was used. It includes blank authoring cards, which reside as in the metaphor of a "stack". Program tools enable the user to design an electronic "stack" which may include video clips, graphics, text and sound. Designers can import graphics, sound, or movie clips from other programs, CDs or the Internet. They can also record their own voices, music and sounds into their stack. The program also offers the designers to view their storyboards, where they can redesign the sequence of any card within each stack.

Data sources

Multiple data sources were used to explore the research questions. These sources included the students' self-reflection journals, observations and interviews, a formative evaluation sheet for evaluation of students' projects and their technical skills.

Journals. At the very beginning of the semester, students were told to keep a journal reflecting their own learning processes and concerns about the issues we discuss throughout the semester. At the very beginning, students were not sure about the concept of journals. The instructor provided guidance on the nature of keeping a journal. The students were told that the journals are different from personal diaries in that these journals would include their beliefs, interests, thoughts and personal concerns about the topics covered in the course.

Observations and interviews. Each class included a computer lab session. These sessions were observed by the instructor and logs were kept by the instructor. In the middle and at the end of the semester, two interview sessions were held both individually with students and with groups about their products. These sessions became part of the data to be analyzed to explore teacher trainees' perspectives on multimedia design and to clarify certain parts and validate their earlier statements in their journals.

Evaluation of students' projects and their technical skills. Students' finished products were evaluated based on pre-determined criteria. The following categories were included in these criteria: (a) structures—links between various contents (b) screen design—how well they applied their readings upon their multimedia products (i.e., providing help menus, credit messages, title, etc.) (c) use of media—the use of graphics, animations, and audio.

Analysis of the data

One of the purposes of this study was to understand the students' perceived usefulness of viewing multimedia design from ELT teacher trainees' perspective. Therefore, journal entries, interview data and classroom observations were analyzed following the guidelines of Miles and Huberman (1994). Folio Views (1998), a text management software, was used to manage, retrieve, code, and analyze the data for further analysis. The data were then sorted and grouped according to the shared themes and relationships. In order to develop and refine the relationships among those categories, analytic induction strategy was applied (Goetz & LeCompte, 1984). The organized data were also triangulated to verify the meaningful and consistent coherence.

Another research question was to determine EFL teacher trainees' socio-cognitive roles as emerging instructional designers in a collaborative project. During the data analysis process, first, the multimedia projects were analyzed based on the certain design issues; then, these findings were triangulated with teacher trainees' journal reflections and interview data.

Findings

All seven teams completed a multimedia product at the end of the project. My project observations documented that the completion process was not a smooth and easy one. First, available computers for students were considerably old and some computers lacked certain multimedia and software features. Secondly, storage was an important problem for students. As they developed sound, animations, and movie clips, students needed to save those files in a separate media; but, this was not possible. The author helped the groups to save their projects on my laptop by using a cross-cable connection.

Learning Logo programming was part of the course syllabus. While this provided them an authentic context, it also limited students' expressions at the beginning. They started to develop simple page screens. As they learned some programming and editing graphics and sound, they started to include them into their projects. As for the nature of CALL and CALL software, each team asked what multimedia was and how they were categorized. As the projects progressed, these questions changed in focus and range. Some students asked questions like how to incorporate animations and interactive movies in their pieces, while others added new questions which were more specific such as "Is designing a web page similar to what we are doing—referring to creating hyperlinks throughout the projects?".

The gathered data were examined to gain a better understanding of EFL teacher trainees' perceived usefulness of designing their own multimedia. The categories suggest storyboarding and group work are the most articulated benefits of working though a multimedia project. Then, teacher trainees' multimedia products were examined in terms of their content and screen functionality. The features applied in these projects were evaluated to observe how individual socio-cognitive roles have emerged during this process and how these roles have contributed to the team product.

Perceived usefulness of multimedia design: Story boarding

Starting from the first week, students were introduced to the concept and the purpose of developing storyboards. Initially, all groups had difficulty understanding and presenting their content on a storyboard, partly because they did not have any earlier experience. The group Digital Success, for example, considered storyboarding as one of the problems they encountered during their design process. During the interview session with group members, Gulin says:

> Preparing a storyboard was very difficult for us because we have never done such a work before. It was our first experience and it was a bit tiring but it was also very enjoyable. (Interview notes: Gulin # 031)

Aynur and Emel also mentioned in their journals that working on their storyboard was a difficult but enjoyable activity for them.

> Forming a storyboard is a hard and amusing activity. We prepared cards and wrote them on little pages and stuck them on a cartoon…[this] was harder than I had expected…however, we laughed very much because we produced very funny ideas when studying on it. (Journal Entry: Emel: # 017)

> Preparing a storyboard was very different work us because it was our first experience, it was a bit tiring but it was also enjoyable since we learned how to use multimedia to teach English. (Journal Entry: Aynur: # 011)

Similarly, Group Tech described their storyboarding process as a "…challenging, time-consuming, and exhausting experience" (Interview notes: Oncel # 013). Another Group Tech member, Ercan, added that "…This project results from a hard study…I enjoyed a lot during the process. We had not only hard time but also a joyful job" (Interview notes: Ercan # 013).

Initially, each group perceived storyboarding as a difficult but an enjoyable task. As they worked through their storyboards, their curiosity was aroused to see how their storyboards would look like when they designed their cards in HyperStudio. During the interview session with Group Tech members, Ercan confessed that he was "…sure it would be wonderful and remarkable to see the results of their storyboard" (Interview notes: Ercan: # 013). In her journal, Gulin also emphasized that: "coming together, sharing ideas, and making decisions on our [storyboard] is enjoyable. I am eager to see the outcome as soon as possible" (Journal Entry: Gulin: # 021).

Students as teacher trainees in the CALL course perceived storyboarding as a useful experience for their future career. For Digital Success, learning how to design a storyboard was a great benefit to be transferred into their future projects. Members of Digital Success say:

> We think we are very lucky because only few people have a CALL course and learn preparing storyboards. We can prepare more detailed, useful projects in

the future by means of what we have learnt and we will use this project when we teach as teachers. (Interview notes: Hacer # 022)

Aynur goes further to add that "when I become a teacher, I can produce multimedia projects so that I can help my students to gain a much greater understanding of the subject. Learning how to prepare a storyboard is a great benefit for us to develop future projects" (Journal Entry: Aynur: # 029).

To sum up, teacher trainees initially perceived the storyboard design process as a difficult and time-consuming task. As they worked through their own projects, either as a group or on an individual basis, they seemed to have fun and enjoyed this process. When they finished their products, they perceived this experience as a valuable skill to be transferred into their future teaching process. Without the help of storyboards, they believed they could not finish their products on time, since storyboards guided them throughout the design process.

Perceived usefulness of multimedia design: Group work

All participants contributed to the final versions of their multimedia piece and their reflections upon group work emerged as a category from the data sources. Working through a task in a timed project required each participant to collaborate with their peers not only during in-class activities, but also during their free time and even at the weekends. Moreover, as students finished their storyboards and started to work on designing their pieces in the computer, they felt that working in a group is much better and they established their roles in the group during group work. Consequently, students expressed great appreciation and the inevitable need to work in a group in order to accomplish the multimedia design tasks on time.

As mentioned earlier, students were given flexibility to choose their own peers to form a group. Choosing a name for the group was an initial step to put students into a group. By the end of the second week, each group had a name. This process clearly indicated that students were making decisions as a group, as members in the group negotiated these names with each other. Aynur's journal entry and Gulin's interview report, for example, are representations of this negotiation and decision making process:

> We thought that it [the group name] should be related to the course and computer. First, we decided that cyberspace is suitable, but we changed it with 'digital success' since we decided to be successful. (Journal Entry: Digital Success: Aynur # 042)

> We were thinking about some names. My idea for the group was merry-go-round. Nonetheless, we have found it a bit childish. Then Anıl [another group member] asked 'what about fish and chips?' It has sounded us a bit funny. And we decided that it should be our group's name. (Interview: Fish and Chips: Gulin # 038)

The process of developing a storyboard had made the groups come together more often. They usually met after the class hours and at the weekends. Those who had computers at home invited the other group members to their apartments, and those who did not met at Internet Cafes. Most of the weekends, the author opened the computer lab at the weekends so that they could come and work at their convenience. These gatherings kept the students together to solve their problems and motivated them for team work. Ercan commented on the benefits of taking this course as follows:

> This course showed me the significance and meaningfulness of group work. None of us could deal with it individually. It was a team work and we've learned how to work as a team. I have learned that we can overcome any difficulty through solidarity and cooperation. (Journal Entry: Ercan # 049)

Upon completing their projects, the students expressed their appreciation and how they benefited from each other while working in a group. Ercan and Ozlem described their experiences as follows:

> I understand that studying on HyperStudio by myself is limited…For example, I did not know that if we drag the animation while pressing the mouse button on it, the animation will go long the way that we drag…I leaned this in my group. (Journal Entry: Ozlem # 063)

Consequently, group work became an integral part of designing a multimedia project as well as a stimulus to better present their final product. As Eda puts it, they were "…not only trying to do their best but also working with a group soul" to complete their projects for presenting their group work to their peers.

Emerging roles in multimedia design process

The process of designing a multimedia product made each class member join in a group and contribute to final products. Initially, some students had preconceived notions about the nature of doing a group work; but, they set their expectations beforehand.

> In group works, generally each student passes the ball to the others. However, this one will not be that kind of work since each student will have a role. Therefore, each student will join the lesson, want to learn more, and be active. (Journal Entry: Gülin # 007)

Inevitably, these expectations led the emergence of certain socio-cognitive roles emerge. Group members put forward their strengths to contribute to the group project. They met with each other during their multimedia development process; they helped each other; they acted on personal relationship to promote group cohesion and accomplishing their tasks. The following table displays group names, selected content, and their intended audience.

Table 1. Group names, multimedia design contents, and intended audience

	Content	Intended Audience
S'CALL'ERS (n=3)	Prepositions	5th Graders
The BEATLES (n=2)	Comparative/Superlatives	4th & 5th Graders
GROUP TECH (n=5)	Quantifiers	8th Graders
DIGITAL SUCCESS (n=5)	Reported Speech	9th Graders
FISH 'N' CHIPS (n=4)	Adjectives/Comparatives	7th Graders
GROUP MONITOR (n=3)	Comparatives	7th Graders
GROUP MOUSE (n= 5)	Simple Present Tense / Simple Past Tense	6th Graders

As indicated in Table 1, groups varied according to the range of topics and grade levels in their design tasks. A comprehensive analysis of all seven final products showed that all groups made an effort to use extensive media. They worked hard to learn develop and integrate various media incorporated with textual data. They also attempted to transfer their readings into their multimedia products. For example, the design characteristics of a multimedia piece as including an index option, title screens, credit messages, and help menu were present in almost all products (See, Figures 1-7 students' final multimedia products).

Language teacher trainees as multimedia designers: Voices from a CALL classroom   95

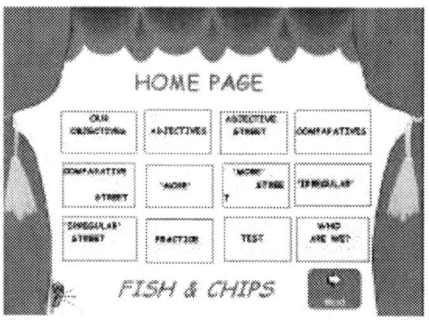

Figure 1 Index (Fish 'n' Chips)

Figure 2 Title page (Digital Success)

Figure 3 Group monitor

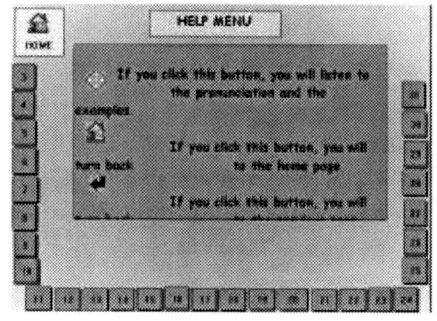

Figure 4 Help menu (Group Tech)

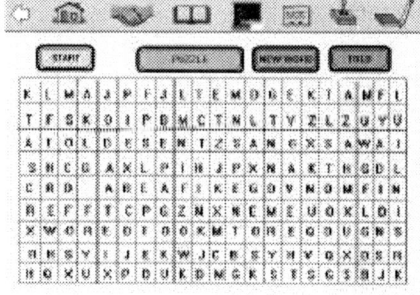

Figure 5 Puzzle (Group Mouse)

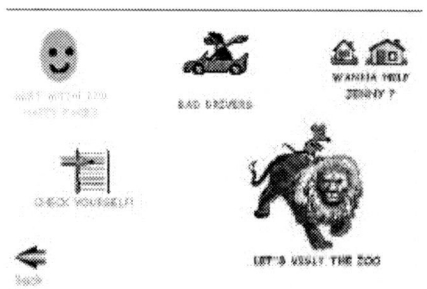

Figure 6 Navigation menu (The Beatles)

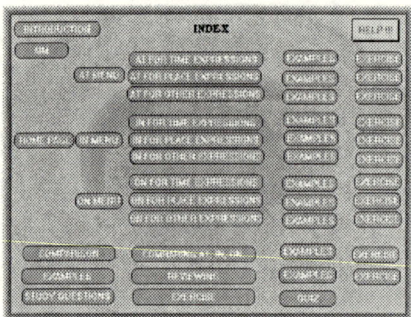

Figure 7 An index menu (Group S'CALL'ers)

Each HyperStudio stack consisted of a set of interrelated screen pages that were linked together with the help of "point and click" buttons and/or objects. The number of created screen pages was different for each design team. In terms of their functionality, three categories were defined as: Information pages, Content pages, and Practice/Feedback pages. Information pages refer to the screens which covered help screens, title pages where participants introduced themselves and credentials, or index pages. Content pages are the ones which displayed the content of the given topic. Practice/Feedback pages, on the other hand, were the screens where students complemented their multimedia with examples, practices and feedback screens. Some feedback screens also included animations and pop-up menus. Since these screens were designed as a separate page (although it looks as if it is on the same page), they were counted as a new page. Table 2 shows the overall proportion of designed screens in the projects.

Since there is a difference among total screen pages, the proportions of each functional unit were converted into percentages. As seen from Table 2, Group the Beatles spent the most of their screens on presenting information. Although Group Mouse developed the highest number of pages in their project, they were equal with group Tech in their percentages of allocating content pages for their audience. Moreover, Group Mouse is the least concern group as far as the feedback and practice screens are concerned.

Table 2. Distribution of screen pages across functionality

	Information page n	%	Content pages n	%	Practice/feedback n	%	Total Screen # n	%
S'CALL'ERS	6	14.6%	27	65.8%	8	19.6%	41	100%
The BEATLES	10	23.2%	22	51.2%	11	25.6%	43	100%
GROUP TECH	3	9.1%	27	81.8%	3	9.1%	33	100%
DIGITAL SUCCESS	7	26%	14	51.8%	6	22.2%	27	100%
FISH 'N' CHIPS	7	17.7%	28	72%	4	10.3%	39	100%
GROUP MONITOR	5	14.7%	23	67.6%	6	17.7%	34	100%
GROP MOUSE	9	11.7%	63	81.8%	5	6.5%	77	100%

A further analysis was done to see how much media (i.e., animations, graphics, and sound) the groups have incorporated into their multimedia stacks. Figure 8 displays the distribution of media use across seven groups.

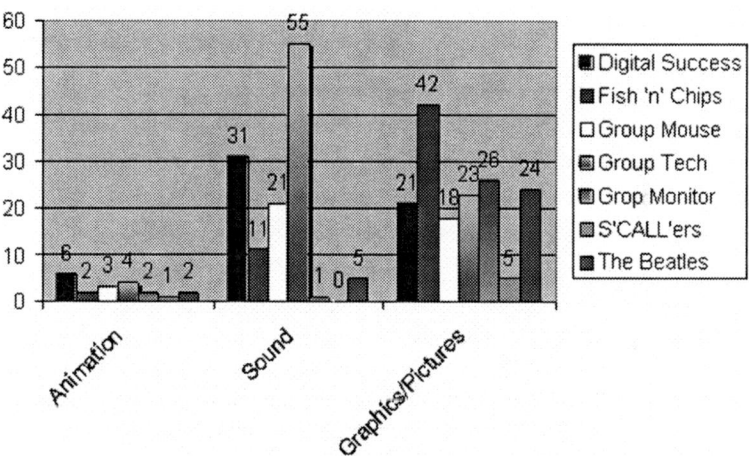

Figure 8 Distribution of media use across groups

As shown in Figure 8, almost all groups used animations, sound and graphic/pictures in their projects. Group Digital Success used animations more than any other group. As far as sound is concerned, Group Tech has the lead; whereas, S'CALL'ers had the least number of media among the others (only 6 different media for a total of 32-page stack). Notably, on the other hand, Group Tech has a total of 82 different media in their 27-page stack.

Team effort and individual contributions are important indicators

In a project-based approach, participants in teams or groups work through their projects with a team effort (McDaniel & Liu, 1996). This process heavily relies on individual differences and collaboration among team members (Liu, 1998). Thus, the differences among the choice of media, number of content and information pages across groups can be attributed to the individual differences and their roles in the design process. The analysis of data in line with these final products revealed four roles: Media Fans, Navigation Builders, Content Developers, and Fun Seekers. These roles represented how the students related to one another in their group work as they worked on their final products.

Media Fans. During the CALL course, the author instructed the students on using a graphic, sound and animation software as well as how these media could be incorporated into HyperStudio. Some students seemed very enthusiastic about these features and spent enormous time in learning and using various software programs. In her journal entry, Eda narrates her appreciation as follows:

> On Tuesday, I went to the Internet Café with Tolga and Gulin. We had to wait for a computer since no was available. This café appeared to me as if they were using computers just for chatting and reading or responding e-mails. Once I sat at a desk, we placed the disk, the picture of me, as a bee, appeared on the screen. What we did was to change the size of picture. Secondly, cut my nose and stick it to my lips. Then, cleared up the hair drawn by us on the previous lesson, later turned upside down and we all laughed. (Journal Entries: Eda # 039)

Clearly, those who were eager to work with media made a difference in their efforts. In Group Mouse, for example, Havacan was the source for recording and incorporating sounds. During the interview session, she said that she was working on recording and digitizing sound at home whenever possible. Since S'CALL'ers produced the least number of media, the author has asked them about their choices during an interview. Fatih, from S'CALL'ers answered:

> We have no sound in their project. When we visited schools, we noticed that they were not using sound cards. We wanted to produce something for computer labs at schools, where there are no sound cards available. (Interview notes: Fatih # 089)

Language teacher trainees as multimedia designers: Voices from a CALL classroom 99

In addition, another group member, Sema added:

> If we were to make this project again, we would like to use more media. If only we had a library of sound, animation, and graphics. (Interview notes: Sema # 058)

In Digital Success, there were two members who took a leading role in developing media. Hale prepared the sound recordings and Aysegul developed the animations. In their final presentation, another group member, Aynur told her classmates that the most enjoyable part of this project was the phase of producing animations.

In a follow-up interview, the author asked the Group Tech members about their use of media-since they have the most extensive use of them. Ercan said:

> Ugur has a computer at home. When we have time Tolga and him worked together with animations and sound. We also helped them. We copied some pictures from the internet, saved them on disk, gave it to Ugur. (Interview notes: Ercan # 088)

To sum up, the groups with media fans and availability of sources for their convenient study had produced more media in quantity than those who did not.

Navigation Builders. All the students in the CALL class were taking such a course for the first time. Navigation, therefore, was a new concept for all of them. As part of the requirement for the course, they needed to do extensive reading on CALL. These readings along with lectures provided them an introductory lesson on navigation and its importance for their users.

Students started to think about navigation and navigational issues for their projects as they worked through their storyboards. As some students focused more on content and media, some students took the role of building navigational links for their group. In group Fish 'n' Chips, Anıl was shown as the navigation builder. According to group members, "…everybody was adding something to the storyboard. As [they] discuss on these new ideas, [they] come up with newer ideas. It is Anıl, who put all these ideas and connect them on the storyboard." (Interview Notes: Group Fish 'n' Chips: Eda # 101).

Although most students contributed equally to their storyboarding, actual incorporation of those links between screen pages was the distinguishing characteristic of navigation builders. A member of Group Mouse, Yurdagul, was another navigation builder in the class. She said it was her responsibility to prepare the practice/feedback section. According to her, classroom readings were helpful for her when designing the pages with links. She said:

> There were many cards in our storyboard. I did not want them placed as they were seen on the books. This made me think a lot. In our class readings, we read that texts are better if accompanied by graphics. I also wanted the users interact with the cards rather than reading from the screen. (Interview Notes: Group Mouse: Yurdagul # 95)

It is clear that the students benefited from classroom readings throughout their learning process. This transfer of knowledge also gave insights to individual designers to better define their roles. Moreover, students as designers discovered more features as they work on adding navigational links to their cards. Yurdagul goes further to add:

> At first, I could only add links to buttons. But I wanted to add links to other objects and texts. I wanted to let the users move to other sections from the homepage. However, it was impossible to squeeze the text on buttons. Later on, I discovered the pen tool to add links. That made me so happy. (Interview Notes: Yurdagul # 82)

Content Developers. One of the emphasized issues in our teacher-training program is the content. Due to the very nature of the CALL course, each group had to decide on a certain content for which they were supposed to develop a multimedia project. Initially, the author asked them to visit a school and consult with a teacher about a topic. In the first three weeks, all groups had made their topics clear and were ready to develop their content.

Some groups had to spend more time on gathering and displaying information compared to other groups. S'CALL'ers emphasizes how they were involved with content design as follows:

> We had to expand one page to ten. What we read about instructional design told us that it was better to have on example on each page. When we were designing the storyboard, we did not think about this. We spent a lot of time with content. I think we had a good one. (Interview Notes: Group S'CALL'ers: Sema # 79)

Content developers did not only go out and bring texts for the projects. They frequently invoked ideas and contributed to the group dynamics with their insightful comments. Moreover, they were pointed out as critical thinkers in the group. In group Fish 'n' Chips, for example, Eda and Gulin were shown as the main contributors. In her journal, Gulin (referring to Eda) wrote:

> We were all trying hard to develop our storyboard. I have really appreciated Gulin for her endless effort to our project. She not only knows her responsibilities but also thinks critically about every detail and situation. I thank for her regular attendance and fresh ideas. (Journal Entries: Gulin # 83)

Anıl, another group member in Fish 'n' Chips, mentioned how Gulin contributed to their content with her new ideas.

> We were browsing through the textbooks for our content. These texts sounded funny to us. All of a sudden, Gulin said we should have two people talk with each other instead of presenting the text. We liked the idea. Eda and Gulin wrote the dialogue, and I recorded it to the computer. (Journal Entry: Anıl # 49)

Another group with an extensive use of content screens was Group Mouse. Nuray, Nilgun and Havacan emphasized that they were mainly responsible for developing the content. According to them, storyboard was a real guide to be able to finish the project on time. They emphasized that each one of them was responsible for one section and they made the entire content ready as they finished their storyboards. Clearly, this promptness and having three members gave this group an advantage to develop more content pages than the others.

Fun Seekers. Multimedia design is known to be a cumbersome process. Moreover, if not planned well, this process can be a never ending story. Thanks to group members, all groups had finished their products on time. One of the reasons for this was the appeal of games and having fun while learning. As some students were swamped with mid-term exams and extensive readings, some enjoyed the playful side of multimedia design. They even took a step further; they contributed to their group projects by adding fun and game-like features.

In their group project, Group Mouse included two games in their design. One was a crossword puzzle and the other one was scrabble. Habibe, a Group Mouse member, mentioned how her mind was boggled with finding such a fun side for their project. She wrote in her journal:

> It is not an easy job to come up with a game which school children would like. I wonder what kind of games they would like to play? I asked these questions to myself many times. I have roommates from the department of

elementary education. I asked them for their opinions, too. (Interview Notes: Group Mouse: Habibe # 68)

Her group members also shared her endeavor for incorporating games in their projects. During the interview, Havacan says:

It was impossible for us to finish what we have now. We cannot think everything. For example, I could not think about including Games as part of the exercises. When Habibe told us about this, we all loved it. (Interview Notes: Group Mouse: Havacan # 65)

The author asked Habibe who worked on putting the puzzle and scrabble in HyperStudio during a follow up interview. She said she mostly worked on it by herself and she spent many hours to understand how to use buttons and transitions to make it happen.

In conclusion, designing game-like environments is a difficult and time-consuming process for novice multimedia designers. Not surprisingly, no other group had produced such game-like exercises. A couple of other students also mentioned that they were thinking of incorporating games in their projects, but they gave up since it is difficult to design it in HyperStudio. Generally speaking, both media fans and content developers enjoyed the feeling of having fun and considered using a computer as a toy. Yet, it is the actual hands-on design which distinguishes fun-seekers from other roles. Therefore, we have only Group Mouse with such game-like feature —with Habibe's personal contributions.

Conclusion

This study was designed to understand ESL/EFL teacher trainees' meaning construction processes during a multimedia design task. The findings suggest that ESL/EFL teacher trainees benefited more from learning how to design a storyboard and join in a group work. They perceived the multimedia design process as a valuable experience to be transferred into their future teaching careers. In addition, four categories of multimedia design roles were suggested: Media Fans, Navigation Builders, Content developers, and Fun Seekers. Having considered that students knew each other for two years by then, they knew whom to choose in forming their groups. Thus, it can be speculated that this flexibility led to the emergence of such roles.

In line with earlier research studies, the findings of this study indicate that teacher trainees improved in their content area understanding and programming skills (see, Kafai, et. al., 1997), mainly due to the available situated contexts (Egbert, Paulus & Nakamichi, 2002). As also suggested by Hanson-Smith (1997), the students became an integral part of their learning experience as they worked in group multimedia projects. Moreover, these projects made significant contributions to language learners' social development as they became masters of one piece of the technology, and then shared their experiences with peers and the teacher (Hanson-Smith, 1997).

Based on observations and analyses, these findings indicate that ESL/EFL teacher trainees' perceptions and experiences do adequately prepare them for their long-term future careers. They all seemed to be willing to integrate CALL related content in their teaching professions, when they were given opportunities. Furthermore, this study also suggests that students can work in a group soul to better prepare a CALL environment for language learners.

There is definitely a need for further research exploring the long-term benefits of how trained students apply their knowledge and skills in school settings. This study was not designed to explore how much language learning occurred during design process; rather, it explored how language learners as teacher trainees perceived the usefulness of multimedia design and developed designer roles. Another study could explore the nature of language learning during multimedia design process. In addition, the dynamics of group formation processes and the effects of peers on group dynamics should be explored in a given context. Moreover, such interaction between learning environments and multimedia design and language learning outcomes as a result of technology integration should be examined from different paradigms.

References

Altun, A. (2003). Understanding hypertext in the context of reading on the Web: Language learners' experience. *Current Issues in Education, 6*(12). Retrieved January 16, 2004, from http://cie.ed.asu.edu/volume6/number12/

Beatty, K. (2003). *Teaching and researching computer-assisted language learning.* London: Pearson Education.

Chapelle, C. A. (1998). Multimedia CALL: Lessons to be learned from research on instructed SLA. *Language Learning & Technology, 2*(1), 22-34. Retrieved December 2, 2003, from http://llt.msu.edu/vol2num1/article1/index.html

Driscoll, M. P. (1984). Alternative paradigms for research in instructional systems. *Journal of instructional development, 7*(4), 2-5.

Egbert, J., Paulus, T. M., & Nakamichi, Y. (2002). The impact of CALL instruction on classroom computer use: A foundation for rethinking technology in teacher education. *Language Learning & Technology, 6*(3), 108-126.

Ellis, R. (1999). Theoretical perspectives on interaction and language learning. In Ellis, R. (Ed.), *Learning a second language through interaction* (pp. 3-31). Amsterdam: John Benjamins Publishing Company.

Folio Views (1998). *Folio Views* (Version 4.11) [Folio Corporation]. Provo: UT.

Fried-Booth, D. L. (1997). *Project work.* (8th Ed.) Oxford: Oxford University Press.

Goetz, J. & LeCompte, M. (1984). *Ethnography and qualitative research design in educational research.* New York: Academic Press.

Hanson-Smith, E. (1997). Multimedia Projects for ESL/EFL Students. *CAELL Journal, 7*(4), 3-13.

Hutchings, G., Hall, W., Briggs, J., Hammond, N., Kibby, M., McKnight, C., & Riley, D. (1992). Authoring and evaluation of hypermedia for education. *Computers and Education, 18*(1-3), 171-177.

Jonassen, D.H., Wilson, B.G., Wang, S., & Grabinger, R.S. (1993). Constructivist uses of expert systems to support learning. *Journal of Computer-Based Instruction, 20*(3), 86-94.

Kafai, Y. B., Carter-Ching, C. & Marshall, S. (1997). Children as designers of educational multimedia software, *Computers & Education, 29*(2-3), 117-126.

Larsen-Freeman, D., & Long, M. (1991). *An introduction to second language acquisition research.* London: Longman.

Lawrence, A. (199). Expanding capacity in ESOL programs (EXCAP): Using projects to enhance instruction. Literacy Harvest: *The Journal of the Literacy Assistance Center, 6*(1), 1-9.

Liu, M. (1998). A study of engaging high-school students as multimedia designers in a cognitive apprenticeship-style learning environment. *Computers in Human Behavior, 14*(3), 387-415.

McDaniel, K. & Liu, M. (1996). A study of project management techniques for developing interactive multimedia programs: A practitioner's perspective. *Journal of Research on Computing in Education, 29*, 29-48.

Miles, M. B. & Huberman, A. M. (1994). *Qualitative Data Analysis* (2nd Ed.). Thousand Oaks, CA: Sage.

Nunan, D. (1999). *Second language teaching and learning.* Boston: Heinle & Heinle.

Pica, T. (1994). Research on negotiation: What does it reveal about second language learning conditions, processes, and outcomes? *Language Learning, 44*(3), 493-527.

Pica, T., Kanagy, R., & Falodun, J. (1993). Choosing and using communication tasks for second language instruction. In G. Crookes, & S. Gass (Eds.), *Tasks and language learning: Integrating theory & practice* (pp. 9-34). Clevedon, England: Multilingual Matters.

Son, J.-B. (2002). Computers, learners and teachers: Teamwork in the CALL classroom. *English Language Teaching, 14*(2), 239-252.

Van Duzer, C., Moss, D. (1998). *Project-based learning for adult English language learners.* Washington, DC: National Clearinghouse for ESL Literacy Education. (ERIC Document Reproduction Service No. ED427556).

Vygotsky, L.S. (1978). *Mind in society.* Cambridge, MA: Harvard University Press.

Warschauer, M., & Healey, D. (1998). Computers and language learning: An overview. *Language Teaching, 31*, 57-71.

Wenden, A. (1991). *Learner strategies for learner autonomy: Planning and implementing learner training for language learners.* Prentice-Hall, Englewood Cliffs, NJ.

Wrigley, H.S. (1998). Knowledge in action: The promise of project-based learning. *Focus on Basics, 2*(D), 13-18.

6

Teacher development in e-learning environments

Jeong-Bae Son

Abstract

With the advance of information and communication technology (ICT) and the growth of interest in the use of the Internet for education, teachers are now working in new online environments. In line with this situation, there is great need for teacher development in the integration of ICT into teaching and learning activities and in the design, implementation and evaluation of e-learning. In productive and practical ways, computer-mediated communication (CMC) can help teachers build and apply their knowledge, collaborate in their learning with fellow teachers, and reflect on their classroom practice. This chapter addresses the issue of how the features of CMC foster teacher development in terms of communication, collaboration and reflection. Examples are taken from CMC activities employed for a computer-assisted language learning (CALL) course in a postgraduate program. It is suggested that teacher development can be effectively promoted by CMC with interactive communication, professional collaboration and critical reflection in situated contexts.

Introduction

Teacher quality has a great impact on student achievement (Albion, 2003; Darling-Hammond, 2000; Pratt, Lai & Munro, 2001). An Australian government report recognises that "education of the highest quality requires teachers of the highest quality" (Department of Education, Science and Training, 2000, p. 1). In improving the quality of teachers, professional development has been identified as a key factor (Pratt, Lai & Munro, 2001). It plays a significant role in ensuring that teachers are able to enhance student learning in their teaching situations.

The Internet, particularly the World Wide Web, provides teachers with a rich and varied teaching environment. Along with a huge increase in schools accessing the Internet, there is a growing recognition that teachers need to be well equipped to meet the challenges of the new online environment. Those challenges are placing pressures on teachers, including the need to develop new skills and strategies required in the use of information and communication technology (ICT) for their teaching. Now, more than ever, teachers are requested to not only know about ICT but also use it for their professional development (Lai, 2001).

The integration of ICT into teaching and learning activities has been recognised by Australian government reports as a key component in teacher professional development (Pearson, 2003). For example, Education Queensland's (2002) professional standards for teachers include teaching and learning strategies that integrate ICT to enhance student learning. The standards are described in the following statements:

- Determine students' learning needs in relation to the use of available information and communication technologies;

- Select learning strategies and resources based on the use of information and communication technologies to cater for students' learning needs and styles;

- Create learning experiences in which students actively use information and communication technologies to organise, research, interpret, analyse, communicate and represent knowledge;

- Evaluate the effectiveness of teaching and learning approaches based on the use of information and communication technologies;

- Use information and communication technology tools to access and manage information on student learning. (Education Queensland, 2002, p. 6)

With the advance of ICT and the growth of interest in e-learning, many institutions are currently offering various online courses that utilise a range of computer-mediated communication (CMC) tools (Trewern & Lai, 2001). These online courses attract students with great flexibility in study time and places. Postgraduate programs offered by universities have particularly been a form of formal professional development for teachers (Albion, 2003), whereas online professional networks or communities have begun to be recognised as a form of informal professional development for teachers (Trewern & Lai, 2001).

This paper explores the importance and role of teacher development and examines how features of CMC influence activities for teacher development and foster communication, collaboration and reflection in online environments. Example practices are taken from an applied linguistics postgraduate course entitled computer-assisted language learning (CALL) offered at a university in Australia. Students who enrol in the course are English as a second/foreign language (ESL/EFL) or language other than English (LOTE) in-service teachers. The course is thus designed to introduce language teachers to the field of CALL by providing them with insights into key aspects of CALL and a basic knowledge of the practical uses of computer technology in language education.

Communication

While changing the way of interpersonal communication, CMC is linking individuals and educational institutions with their counterparts in other locations. A number of researchers have looked at various aspects of CMC such as academic writing in computer conferencing (Durham, 1990), flaming behaviour (Lea, O'Shea, Fung & Spears, 1992), intercultural communication (Ma, 1996), interactions in conventional university courses (Light, Colbourn & Light, 1997; Light & Light, 1999; Light, Nesbitt, Light & Burns, 2000; Warren & Rada, 1998), online chat and group-work (Pilkington, Bennett & Vaughan, 2000), tutor group in distance education (Weller, 2000), distance students' online behaviour (Wilson & Whitelock, 1997, 1998), and teacher education (Ahern & El-Hindi, 2000; Schlagal, Trathen & Blanton, 1996; Trentin, 1997). As noted in these studies, CMC is utilised in a wide range of educational settings in the form of e-mail, text chatting, voice chatting, video conferencing, electronic discussion groups or Web-based bulletin boards (Son, 2002).

The aforementioned CALL course strongly encourages teachers to participate in various kinds of online communication activities. An online discussion group established for the course, in particular, allows teachers to post their own answers to pre-selected questions/tasks given in their Study Book and to feel free to make comments on fellow teachers' answers. Son (2002) reports that, apart from tasks given as course requirements, topics brought up and discussed actively by participants themselves in the discussion group included the printing press, the quality of teachers, information technology (IT) skills and language learners, keyboard skills, and writing on the computer. For instance, one of the most interactive discussions was initiated by a teacher's interest and opinion on writing assignments on the computer. Through postings to the discussion group, other teachers described their habits and preferences in using word processing programs and expressed their views on the use of computers in the second language classroom.

While giving an idea of what types of interactions can be anticipated in text-based synchronous communication, on the other hand, the following example log demonstrates interactive discussions and exchange of opinions occurred in a text chat meeting for the CALL course.

> ...
> <N> My problem as a teacher is that its a devil of a job even getting a class into our computer lab at the moment.
> <N> Time constraints both is preparation (for the teacher) and then lab use really restrict this kind of activity for my students
> <S> agreed—I sometimes wonder whether the learning curve is worth it
> <J-B> Yes, that is one of the biggest problems the language teacher has.
> <S> we all need more time and bigger salaries...
> <N> I have noticed that more and more students are more confident and competent with using computers these days though
> <N> I know my school realises that we do have to increase computer numbers and continue to upgrade etc
> <S> the trouble is schools often buy computers and no-one can take care of them
> <N> We have a computer guru who is terrific
> <S> you are really lucky—without a guru, you can have a lot of problems.
> <S> I'm a Macintosh guru but haven't got the faintest idea about windows
> <N> I tend to use the computer more for word processing with my EAP students
> <S> how many students in a class
> <N> 12-14
> <Ae> I would like to flag that for me despite the advances of the internet I still find it frustratingly slow, ie loading sites etc,
> Anonymous33 has joined the chat room.
> <Ae> isn't it also like this for students?
> <S> yes, surfing is a myth....
> <S> I love the term the world wide wait.
> <Ae> excellent!
> ...

It is certain that the widespread use of CMC raises the significance of effective communication skills (Warschauer, 2001). As shown in the examples above, CMC activities offer an interactive learning environment that can foster the acquisition of communicative skills.

Collaboration

The quality of teachers can be enhanced when teachers engage professionally in collaborative learning (Albion, 2003; Pratt, Lai & Munro, 2001). CMC has great potential to foster collaboration connected to the real world. The following postings to the discussion group for the CALL course show that a teacher's answer to a question could generate other teachers' responses to the answer accompanied by follow-up interactions and allow them to collaborate in building and applying knowledge.

> Q: What benefits do you see in using electronic mail in second language teaching?
>
> > One of the greatest benefits, in my opinion, is access to native speakers in a relaxed environment. There is no pressure for participants in the email exchange to respond immediately. They have time to read, reflect and then reply.
>
> This kind of activity also allows for increased cross-cultural awareness, when using authentic language and socio-cultural references.
>
> I also think student motivation to study the L2 and learn more about the target culture increases, as students engage in purposeful, communicative language activities. They are really communicating with someone from the target culture and being understood.
>
> On the negative side, it is easy for students to opt out of the learning activity if they feel their language skills are not good enough, or they lack confidence.
>
> K
>
> >> Hello K,
>
> I agree with your statement that "They have time to read, reflect and then reply." when using e-mail for CALL. Would you also agree that the lack of pressure to respond enables students to edit and to make sure there are no mistakes?

Another point that I thought would be necessary is that teachers should prepare students adequately enough in order for them to be sensitive to cultural and social differences when dealing with the target country.

I know for a fact that an e-mail activity that was left too open-ended by the teacher, or if an any-subject was allowed it could turn negative. Here in 00, males should not interact with females even in e-mail, and discussion about some current events that are on every student's mind could lead to more misunderstandings.

My question is this: Will students be prepared enough to use authentic language and proper socio-cultural references? A lack of education and respect for the target countries differences could be beyond the ability of the students and could lead to problems.

I'm really not so negative, but these are some considerations that teachers have to be aware of and guidance from a CALL instructor is once again crucial.

P

>>> Hello P,

I recall speculating about such complexities of communicating in an intercultural setting in a previous posting (#1.3.4, 27 Mar). The non-native speaker requires not only the linguistic and sociolinguistic knowledge of the target language, but also knowledge of the culture and the cultural rules which impact greatly on the choice of content and the process of communicative interaction which is meaningful in particular contexts.

I agree with the need for cultural awareness and guidance on the part of a CALL instructor. It's a rather daunting task as this presents a huge challenge to address the many differences in learners' interpretations, perceptions, definitions of linguistic forms, as well as the need to consider native speakers' different value judgements and perceptions of "appropriate formality, intensity, directness, register, politeness, taboo and different pragmatic ground rules"(Thomas, 1983; Olshtain and Blum-Kulka, 1985; Odlin, 1989 in Hudson, Detmer & Brown, 1992, p.6), within a CALL environment.

Regards,

S

Teacher development programs need to encourage teachers to engage in collaborative knowledge building (Albion, 2003). As illustrated above, this engagement in collaborative learning can be well supported by CMC activities such as asynchronous online discussions.

Reflection

Reflective practice encourages teachers to engage in a process of critical reflection on their own teaching and learning experiences. In a review of language teacher education, Crandall (2000) notes, "Long ignored, teacher inquiry and reflection are now viewed as important to the development of language teaching theory and appropriate language teacher education" (p. 40).

In the language teacher education literature (e.g., Kullman, 1998; Richards, 1998; Roberts, 1998), Dewey's (1910, 1933) ideas on reflective thinking and Schön's (1983, 1987) views of knowing-in-action, reflection-on-action and reflection-in-action have been much discussed in relation to the origins of reflective practice. Based on Dewey's notion of reflection, Bartlett (1990) suggests a cycle for the process of reflective teaching containing five elements of mapping, informing, contesting, appraising, and acting. Wallace (1991), on the other hand, adapts Schön's concept of reflective practitioners and proposes a reflective mode of professional education/development which highlights "the continuing process of reflection on 'received knowledge' and 'experiential knowledge' in the context of professional action (practice)" (p. 56). While pointing out that the focus of the discussions of teacher reflectivity has been given to "the definitions of reflection, the processes of reflection, and, most recently, the investigation of evidence of reflection" (p. 584), Stanley (1998) also proposes a framework for reflective teaching practice in terms of five phases: engaging with reflection; thinking reflectively; using reflection; sustaining reflection; and practicing reflection. In a discussion on the implementation of reflective practice in adult ESL settings, additionally, Florez (2001) summarizes that benefits of reflective practice include flexibility, practicality, professionalism, and sustainability.

Tsui, Wu & Sengupta (1996) describes a computer network called *TeleNex* and asserts that the network provides a platform for teachers to share their reflections with their peers as autonomous professionals. In a study of mentor training in Hungary, Kullman (1998) emphasises that mentors need to help student teachers develop reflective practice. Through an investigation of reflective practice of three experienced EFL teachers in Korea, Farrell (1999) sees the formation of teacher development groups as a good way of promoting reflective practice for teachers and makes five suggestions for future ESL/EFL teacher development groups: (1) join a group of ESL/EFL teachers; (2) build in some ground rules; (3) make provisions for three different kinds of time (time-individual, time-development, and time-frame); (4) provide external input; and (5) provide for a low affective state (pp. 167-170). For a discussion of evidence of reflection, Liou (2001) describes reflective practice of 22 pre-service teachers in Taiwan. Similarly to Farrell's study, she consulted Ho and Richards' (1993) categorisation of descriptive and critical reflection in the analysis of the data collected from 40 written reports and found that her student teachers talked about topics mainly related to teaching, could do more critical reflection than descriptive reflection in observation reports and practice teaching reports, but did not show substantial development of critical reflection over a six-week period.

In online environments, CMC is increasingly considered as a means of providing opportunities for teachers to discuss and facilitate reflective practice (Johnson & Brine, 2000; Kamhi-Stein, 2000; Motteram & Teague, 2000; Nunan, 1999; Son, 2002; Wolcott, 1995). The text below exemplifies three teachers' reflections shown in postings to the discussion group for the CALL course.

> (A) My use of the computer in the classroom: I have taken a piece-meal approach, with a view to gradually building up my repertoire of activities. I have worked with Year 8 students on basic word-processing skills such as cutting and pasting into a word document from an Internet site. I have used the Internet with all ages but especially with Year 11s and 12s. I have devised language various activities based on its use, including reading and listening practice. Sometimes we just use it for fun—e.g. look up the latest film reviews or details of French TV soapies. There are some good language learning sites too, even some that correspond with our textbooks. We have some CD-ROMS that include games, vocabulary activities, simple conversation practice, but we don't have enough site licences for them, and we've had a few technical problems too. I'm not well-informed about the software that's available. I mostly rely on recommendations from other teachers. It's not usually possible to buy software on inspection, which puts me off buying. I don't like to buy without having had a chance to evaluate the product. I've started trying to network with other teachers, mainly through a language teacher association, to find out what the best quality materials are for languages learning.
>
> (B) To be honest, I'm not very proud of my uses of computers for language learning to date. Prior to commencing my studies at USQ, I taught myself

how to make a web-site and developed one to use with my courses. But studies have kept me from updating it and developing the features that I really was hoping to include, such as interactive games and study activities. I downloaded Hot Potatoes software last year and tried to make some exercises, but didn't have time to finish any yet. Consequently, my site is the worst of the worst, primarily posting some tips and class notes for students with very little interactivity. In my defence, however, I have used email and web assignments with my students and will likely be increasing these. In addition, my site has links to interactive learning sites. My students seem to use my website to learn more about me and to communicate with me, but not necessarily for study purposes. I hope this class will give me skills that will help me make it more effective and interesting to increase student use of it. I want to use computers to increase student communication through authentic English, including teacher-student, student-student, and student-world!

(C) I have a variety of experience with computer technology, both personal and professional. I am very ready to take the plunge into further exploring computer use for student learning. In my daily life, I have used and continue to access word processing, e-mail, the WWW and CD-ROM programs on a very regular (often daily) basis. In teaching I use the computer in many ways; record keeping, power point presentations (mainly to colleagues in in-service), and e-mail (both my previous and present schools are working toward using electronic communication over other means). I have also trialled some software programs—mainly Reading, writing and spelling programs for native English speaking children and some drill and practice Math software. As indicated above, I have been very fortunate to work in 'computer literate' environments where a large portion of the budget has been allocated to making computers accessible to both teachers and students. This has included (and continues to) 'in-house' professional development using school-based staff paid for their computing expertise and experience. This course is the perfect opportunity for me to increase my knowledge of what is 'out there' while providing an incentive for my time spent 'playing' and 'exploring'!

These example postings show the teachers' reflection of the ways in which they have used the computer and/or hope to be involved with computers in language teaching. Like this, asynchronous discussion forums can be designed as learning activities to maximise reflection. Delayed-time communication deepens reflection by giving teachers time to think, reflect and then respond to others' views or comments.

Online community

The Internet opens up opportunities not only for situated and collaborative learning but also for building online learning communities (Lai, 2001). Professionally oriented networks can create knowledge-rich communities of practice (Blunt, 2001). Trewern and Lai (2001) indicate, "Groups of teachers can get together and make use of communications technologies to access teaching resources, source new ideas, use communications technologies to share ideas or innovative teaching practices, and reflect on aspects of classroom practice" (p. 45). Online communities can provide teachers with opportunities for ongoing learning in professional manners.

In this respect, it is worth noting that an online association called the Asia-Pacific Association for Computer-Assisted Language Learning (APACALL: http://www.apacall.org/) was established for CALL researchers and practitioners who are willing to investigate, share information, discuss, cooperate and collaborate with fellow professionals. It acts as a clearinghouse for language professionals who are interested in investigating, sharing information, discussing, cooperating and collaborating with fellow professionals working with CALL. The association acknowledges the opportunity for use of information and communication technologies in learning, teaching and research. The introduction of this online association to the world of CALL has been welcomed by many language professionals (e.g., Colpaert, 2002).

APACALL aims to provide a mechanism for information exchange on CALL; highlight the importance and value of accessibility and professional engagement with CALL for teachers, students, researchers and other interested professionals; and promote and support research and good practice in CALL. It endeavours to contribute to the discussion of the impact of CALL on language learning/teaching and development of authentic cross-cultural communications; promote language teacher development in CALL; encourage online activities for CALL practice; promote research and research findings on CALL; facilitate the use of CALL for language program accessibility and flexibility, ongoing language maintenance and cross-cultural exchange; and promote the study of computer-assisted second language acquisition, particularly in the Asia-Pacific region.

Its free membership is open to anyone who is interested in CALL. All members are given opportunities for communication, collaboration and reflection through professional development activities (e.g., interactive discussions, mainly through the APACALL E-list; collaborative projects such as the publication of an APACALL Book Series; online meetings with instant messengers; academic conferences; etc.). With encouragement and ongoing self-discovery, the members themselves find ways of working in the online community and take advantage of CMC-based activities for their own personal and professional development.

Practice

Given the nature of the Internet, e-learning is flexible, interactive and dynamic. Teacher development activities in online environments should be flexible, interactive and dynamic enough to allow teachers to achieve a high degree of personal and professional development. They should be based on interactive communication, professional collaboration and critical reflection in situated contexts.

It is an important task for teachers to develop their competencies in e-learning. CMC plays an important role in e-learning practices and makes a significant contribution to online teacher development. In using CMC tools for the implementation of e-learning, teachers need to:

- explore current development and use of CMC;
- choose appropriate CMC tools;
- learn how to use the tools confidently;
- test and evaluate the tools critically; and
- use the tools in ways that maximize learning.

Online teaching practices will allow teachers to engage in the tasks listed above. Through a practical approach to the use of CMC, teachers will be able to make use of all the tools available to them in order to achieve their developmental goals. Best e-learning practices will likely be put into action by best e-teachers utilising CMC tools effectively and efficiently.

Conclusion

Teachers need to take responsibility for their own professional development. Influenced by the revolution in ICT, e-learning environments demand teachers to be aware of ways of using ICT to improve student learning. Recent online education supports developmental and innovative approaches to professional practice through communication, collaboration and reflection that can enhance teacher development. CMC can help teachers improve their knowledge and collaborate in their learning with fellow teachers. Through such practical experience in online interactions, teachers develop their ability to use CMC tools and communicate with other teachers for their professional development. Importantly, a range of CMC tools are available to teachers, waiting to be explored and used for learning and teaching.

References

Ahern, T., & El-Hindi, A. E. (2000). Improving the instructional congruency of a computer-mediated small group discussion: A case study in design and delivery. *Journal of Research on Computing in Education, 32*, 385-401.

Albion, P. (2003, June). *Exploring online approaches in a revised Master of Education program.* Paper presented in the Brown Bag Seminar Series of the Office of Preparatory and Academic Support, The University of Southern Queensland.

Bartlett, L. (1990). Teacher development through reflective teaching. In J. Richards, & D. Nunan (Eds.), *Second language teacher education* (pp. 202-214). New York: Cambridge University Press.

Blunt, R. (2001). How to build an e-learning community. *Learning & Training Innovations Magazine.* Retrieved February 12, 2003, from the World Wide Web: http://www.elearningmag.com/ltimagazine/article/articleDetail.jsp?id=5040

Colpaert, J. (2002). The world of CALL [Editorial]. *Computer Assisted Language Learning, 15*, 437-439.

Crandall, A. (2000). Language teacher education. *Annual Review of Applied Linguistics, 20*, 34-55.

Darling-Hammond, L. (2000). Teacher quality and student achievement: a review of state policy evidence. *Education Policy Analysis Archives, 8* (1). Retrieved February 12, 2003, from the World Wide Web: http://epaa.asu.edu/epaa/v8n1/

Department of Education, Science and Training (2000). *Teachers for the 21st century—Making the difference*. Retrieved February 12, 2003, from the World Wide Web: http://www.detya.gov.au/schools/Publications/2000/t21.htm

Dewey, J. (1910). *How we think*. Boston, DC: Heath & Co.

Dewey, J. (1933). How we think. Reprinted in W. B. Kolensnick (Ed.). (1958). *Mental discipline in modern education*. University of Wisconsin Press, Madison.

Durham, M. (1990). Computer conferencing, students' rhetorical stance and the demands of academic discourse. *Journal of Computer Assisted Learning, 6*, 265-272.

Education Queensland (2002). *Professional standards for teachers: Guidelines for professional practice*. Retrieved February 12, 2003, from the World Wide Web: http://education.qld.gov.au/learning_ent/ldf/standards/profstandards.pdf

Farrell, T.S.C. (1999). Reflective practice in an EFL teacher development group. *System, 27*, 157-172.

Florez, M.C. (2001). *Reflective teaching practice in adult ESL settings*. Washington, DC: National Clearinghouse for ESL Literacy Education. (ERIC Digest). Retrieved February 12, 2003, from the World Wide Web: http://www.cal.org/ncle/digests/reflect.htm

Ho, B., & Richards, J. C. (1993). Reflective thinking through teacher journal writing: myths and realities. *Prospect, 8*, 7-24.

Johnson, E. M., & Brine, J. W. (2000). Design and development of CALL courses in Japan. *CALICO Journal, 17*, 251-268.

Kamhi-Stein, L. D. (2000). Looking to the future of TESOL teacher education: Web-based bulletin board discussions in a methods course. *TESOL Quarterly, 34*, 423-455.

Kullman, J. (1998). Mentoring and the development of reflective practice: Concepts and context. *System, 26*, 471-484.

Lai, K.-W. (2001). Professional development: too little, too generic? In K.-W. Lai (Ed.), *e-Learning: Teaching and professional development with the Internet* (pp. 7-19). Dunedin: The University of Otago Press.

Lea, M., O'Shea, T., Fung, P., & Spears, R. (1992). 'Flaming' in computer-mediated communication: Observations, explanations, implications. In M. Lea (Ed.), *Contexts of computer-mediated communication* (pp. 89-109). London: Harvester Wheatsheaf.

Light, P., Colbourn, C., & Light, V. (1997). Computer mediated tutorial support for conventional university courses. *Journal of Computer Assisted Learning, 13*, 228-235.

Light, P., & Light, V. (1999). Analysing asynchronous learning interactions: Computer-mediated communication in a conventional undergraduate setting. In K. Littleton, & P. Light (Eds.), *Learning with computers: Analysing productive interaction* (pp. 162-178). London: Routledge.

Light, V., Nesbitt, E., Light, P., & Burns, J. R. (2000). 'Let's you and me have a little discussion': Computer mediated communication in support of campus-based university courses. *Studies in Higher Education, 25* (1), 85-96.

Liou, H.-C. (2001). Reflective practice in a pre-service teacher education program for high school English teachers in Taiwan, ROC. *System, 29*, 197-208.

Ma, R. (1996). Computer-mediated conversations as a new dimension of intercultural communication between East Asian and North American college students. In S. C. Herring (Ed.), *Computer-mediated communication: Linguistic, social and cross-cultural perspectives* (pp. 173-185). Philadelphia: John Benjamins.

Motteram, G., & Teague, J. (2000, April). *"Deep" learning and computer mediated communication: A case study of on-line teacher education.* Paper presented at the Networked Learning 2000 Conference, Lancaster University, UK. Retrieved February 12, 2003, from the World Wide Web: http://collaborate.shef.ac.uk/nlpapers/Teague & Motteram-p.html

Nunan, D. (1999). A foot in the world of ideas: Graduate study through the Internet. *Language Learning & Technology, 3* (1), 52-74. Retrieved February 12, 2003, from the World Wide Web: http://llt.msu.edu/vol3num1/nunan/index.html

Pearson, J. (2003). Information and communications technologies and teacher education in Australia. *Technology, Pedagogy and Education, 12* (1), 39-58.

Pilkington, R., Bennett, C., & Vaughan, S. (2000). An evaluation of computer mediated communication to support group discussion in continuing education. *Educational Technology & Society, 3* (3). Retrieved February 12, 2003, from the World Wide Web: http://ifets.ieee.org/periodical/vol_3_2000/d10.html

Pratt, K., Lai, K.-W., & Munro, P. (2001). Professional development for ICT-using teachers. In K.-W. Lai (Ed.), *e-Learning: Teaching and professional development with the Internet* (pp. 21-36). Dunedin: The University of Otago Press.

Richards, J. C. (1998). *Beyond training.* Cambridge: Cambridge University Press.

Roberts, J. (1998). *Language teacher education.* London: Arnold.

Schlagal, B., Trathen, W., & Blanton, W. (1996). Structuring telecommunications to create instructional conversations about student teaching. *Journal of Teacher Education, 47,* 175-183.

Schön, D. A. (1983). The reflective practitioner: How professionals think in action. London: Temple Smith.

Schön, D. A. (1987). Educating the reflective practitioner: Toward a new design for teaching and learning in the professions. San Francisco: Jossey Bass.

Son, J.-B. (2002). Online discussion in a CALL course for distance language teachers. *CALICO Journal, 20,* 127-144.

Stanley, C. (1998). A framework for teacher reflectivity. *TESOL Quarterly, 32,* 584-591.

Taylor, J. C. (2001). *5th generation distance education* (Higher Education Series Report No. 40). Canberra, Australia: Department of Education, Training and Youth Affairs (DETYA).

Trentin, G. (1997). Telematics and on-line teacher training: The POLARIS Project. *Journal of Computer Assisted Learning, 13*, 261-270.

Trewern, A., & Lai, K.-W. (2001). Online learning: An alternative way of providing professional development for teachers. In K.-W. Lai (Ed.), *e-Learning: Teaching and professional development with the Internet* (pp. 37-55). Dunedin: The University of Otago Press.

Tsui, A. B. M., Wu, K., & Sengupta, S. (1996). Enhancing teacher development through TeleNex—A computer network for English language teachers. *System, 24*, 461-476.

Wallace, M. (1991). *Training foreign language teachers: A reflective approach.* Cambridge: Cambridge University Press.

Warren, K. J., & Rada, R. (1998). Sustaining computer-mediated communication in university courses. *Journal of Computer Assisted Learning, 14*, 71-80.

Warschauer, M. (2001). Millennialism and media: Language, literacy, and technology in the 21st century. *AILA Review, 14*, 49-59.

Weller, M. (2000). Implementing a CMC tutor group for an existing distance education course. *Journal of Computer Assisted Learning, 16*, 178-183.

Wilson, T., & Whitelock, D. (1997). Monitoring a CMC environment created for distance learning. *Journal of Computer Assisted Learning, 13*, 253-260.

Wilson, T., & Whitelock, D. (1998). Monitoring the on-line behaviour of distance learning students. *Journal of Computer Assisted Learning, 14*, 91-99.

Wolcott, L. L. (1995). The distance teacher as reflective practitioner. *Educational Technology, 34* (1), 39-43.

7

Using text chat to improve willingness to communicate

Lily K.L. Compton

Abstract

This study investigates the potential impact of online text chat on learners' willingness to communicate and state communicative self-confidence. Five male international teaching assistants from China were selected as participants to see if the chat experience helped to reduce their state anxiety and increase their state self-perceived competence so that they felt willing to participate in class discussions. The findings showed that the impact of text chat varies from learner to learner and is dependent on variables like topic of discussion and partner's attitude. Willingness to communicate appears to be higher after the chat experience if learners managed to obtain useful information during the chat discussion. An increase in state communicative self-confidence is the result of an increase in state self-perceived competence rather than a decrease in state anxiety. In general, learners found that the chat experience allowed them time to organize their thoughts and provided them with the necessary vocabulary to express their thoughts, making them confident enough to participate in the speaking task.

Introduction

Asynchronous communication (e-mails, bulletin/message boards) and synchronous communication (IRC, MOOs, MUDs[1]) have been used in several studies (Chun, 1994; DiMatteo, 1991; Mabrito, 1992; Pellettieri, 2000; Selfe, 1990)

---

1. IRCs, MOOs and MUDs are virtual social environments utilizing real-time communication. For more information about the different characteristics of each environment, refer to Turbee (1999).

pertaining to teaching writing/composition, increasing student participation, and improving grammatical competence in second/foreign language classrooms. Interestingly, while no specific research on computer-assisted language learning (CALL) has investigated the use of these programs and software to improve speaking skills, the assumption seems to exist that synchronous communication, particularly chatting, is likely to improve one's speaking ability due to the strong resemblance between chatting and speaking. According to Chun (1994),

> since these types of sentences [in the chat discourse] strongly resemble what would be said in a spoken conversation, the hope that the written competence gained from CACD [Computer-Assisted Classroom Discourse] can gradually be transferred to the students' speaking competence as well. (p. 29)

Similarly, Pellettieri (2000) says that,

> because synchronous NBC [Network-based Communication], such as chatting, bears a striking resemblance to oral interaction, it seems logical to assume that the language practice through NBC will reap some of the benefits for second language development as practice through oral interaction. (p. 59)

Having the technology alone is insufficient to address the problems faced by the learners in a speaking classroom. Essentially, learners avoid speaking in class because they are afraid to be seen grappling with words or feel embarrassed with their inadequate ability to construct sentences or express themselves. Some studies (Cheng, Horwitz, and Schallert, 1999; Horwitz, Horwitz, and Cope, 1986; MacIntyre and Gardner, 1991; Schlenker and Leary, 1985; Young, 1991) have attributed this apprehension to language anxiety, which is affected by the learners' level of self-confidence. This study was therefore designed to investigate the impact of CALL, specifically the impact of text chat on learners' self-confidence and willingness to communicate orally.

Learners' hesitation to speak

Hesitation to speak in second language (L2) or foreign language-classrooms often leads to poor improvement in L2 speaking competence. Yet, some language learners avoid speaking in class. In an English as a Second Language (ESL) course emphasizing speaking and presentation skills at a large American university, this reluctance to engage in oral communication is common. The students avoided participation in class discussions even though they knew that their purpose in that class was to improve their speaking skills.

Studies examining language anxiety and speaking (Cheng, 1998; Clément, Gardner & Smythe, 1980; Clément & Kruidenier, 1985; Cohen & Norst, 1989; Daly & Wilson, 1983; MacIntyre, Noels & Clément, 1997; Price, 1991) have reported that low self-confidence and self-perceived competence are the key components to the learners' unwillingness to communicate. These studies consistently found that high levels of language anxiety and low self-perception of competence contributed to low self-confidence.

Cheng, Horwitz, and Schallert (1999) claim that L2 classroom anxiety has a strong speaking anxiety element. Horwitz, Horwitz, and Cope (1986) and MacIntyre and Gardner (1991) support this view, citing listening and speaking as the main sources of anxiety. Young (1991) lists some obvious manifestations of this anxiety that include "the form of distortion of sounds, inability to reproduce the intonation and rhythm of the language, 'freezing up' when called on to perform, and forgetting words or phrases just learned or simply refusing to speak or remaining silent" (p. 430).

Horwitz, Horwitz, and Cope (1986) and Schlenker and Leary (1985) believe that the frustration faced by students attempting to communicate, leads to apprehension about future attempts that cause students to avoid classroom participation. Yet many language teachers "have encountered students high in linguistic competence who are unwilling to use their L2 for communication whereas other students, with only minimal linguistic knowledge, seem to communicate in the L2 whenever possible" (MacIntyre, Clément, Dörnyei, and Noels, 1998, p. 545). This indicates that the level of communicative competence alone does not determine spontaneous and continuous use of L2. MacIntyre, et al. argue that willingness to seek out communication opportunities and willingness to use the L2 should be the ultimate goal of any language learning process so that learners would be able to progress beyond the classroom. Here, they define willingness to communicate (WTC) as "a readiness to enter into discourse at a particular time with a specific person or persons, using a L2" (p. 547). According to MacIntyre, et al., the opportunity to communicate is not absolutely necessary to possess WTC. For example, if several students raise their hands but only one student is selected to verbalize the answer, then all the students who have raised their hands have expressed WTC. Therefore, WTC includes nonverbal communicative events such as hand-raising and unsuccessful attempts to take a turn or respond to someone's comments.

They identify state communicative self-confidence as one variable affecting WTC. This variable is influenced by the state anxiety and state self-perceived competence. Here, the word *state* in these three constructs refers to momentary and transient feelings within a given situation, i.e. speaking in L2. Figure 1 illustrates the relationship between state anxiety and state communicative self-confidence where a high level of state anxiety will lead to a low level of state communicative self-confidence while a low level of state anxiety will lead to a high level of state communicative self-confidence. Figure 1 also illustrates how the state self-perceived competence relates to the state communicative self-confidence. If one's level of state self-perceived competence is high, then the level of state communicative self-confidence will be high. On the contrary, a low level of state self-perceived competence will lead to a low level of state communicative self-confidence. MacIntyre, et al. propose that learners with higher state communicative self-confidence will be more willing to communicate at a particular moment because they believe they are able to express themselves effectively and they are not nervous or worried about making mistakes during their attempt to communicate.

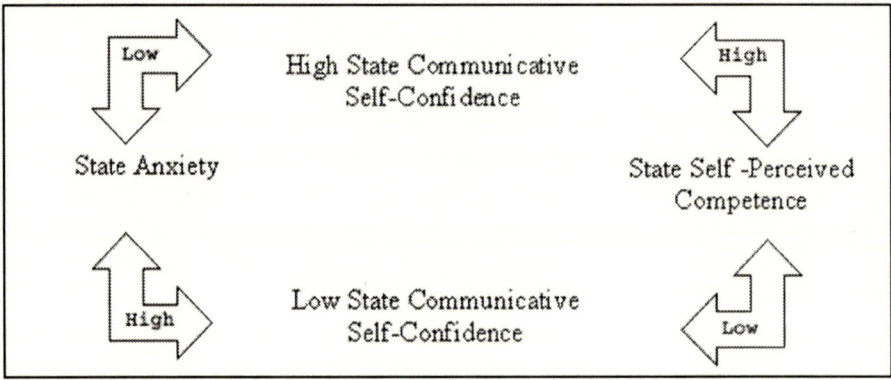

Figure 1 Factors affecting state communicative self-confidence

Figure 2 illustrates the relationships between state anxiety, state self-perceived competence and state communicative self-confidence, and how these relationships can affect the WTC, which then affects the improvement in L2 speaking competence. The increase in state self-perceived competence will lead to an increase in state communicative self-confidence. When learners feel self-confident at a particular moment, they will be willing to speak, and the more they attempt to speak in the L2, the more likely their L2 speaking competence will improve. As they continue to see improvement in their own speaking ability, they will be more willing to seek out opportunities to communicate, reinforcing the increase in their state communicative self-confidence, which then leads to lower levels of state anxiety and higher levels of state self-perceived competence.

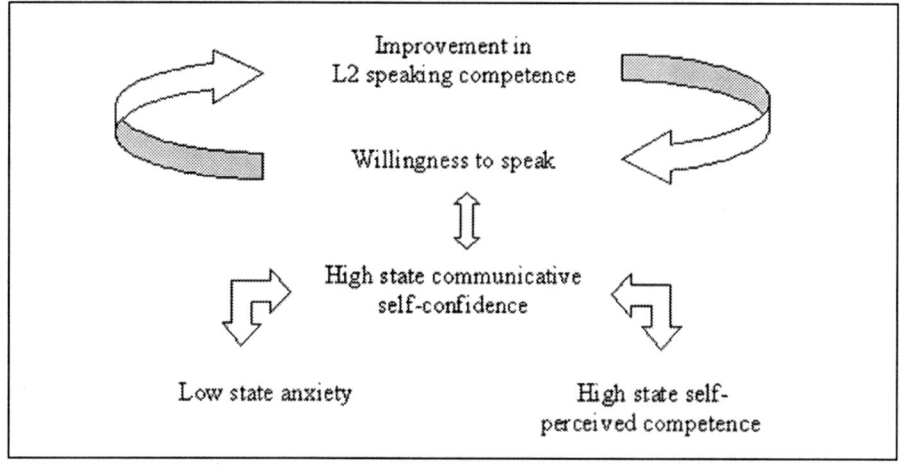

Figure 2 Factors influencing the improvement of speaking skills

The relationships among the constructs in Figure 2 unveil a problem. If students are required to practice speaking in order to improve their L2 speaking competence, they must first be willing to speak. However, if their state self-confidence is low due to high state anxiety and low state self-perceived competence, they may simply refuse to speak or remain silent, which in turn affects their speaking improvement, as shown in Figure 3.
Consequently, a vicious cycle begins, as pointed out by MacIntyre, Noels & Clément (1997),

If language learners do not choose to communicate, they cannot re-assess their competence. Thus begins a vicious cycle, wherein the anxiety level remains high because the anxious student does not accept evidence of increasing proficiency that might reduce anxiety. (p. 278)

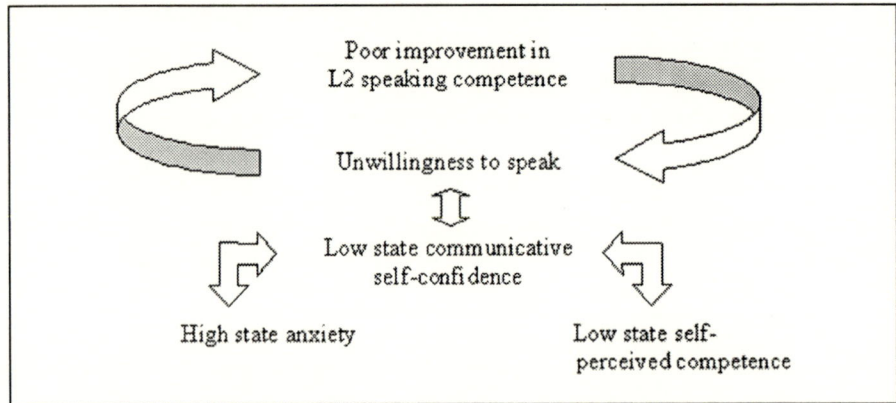

Figure 3 Factors influencing the poor improvements in L2 speaking competence

Therefore, if we wish to ensure that students are able to make progress in their speaking abilities, steps should be taken to minimize their state anxiety and increase their state self-perceived competence so as to ensure their willingness to seek out communication opportunities and willingness to use the L2 as stressed by MacIntyre, et al., (1998). This present study will attempt to investigate whether chat experiences can help to increase learners' WTC and improve state communicative self-confidence. The following research questions were asked: (a) Are learners more willing to communicate after chatting? (b) Do learners who have participated in chat tasks feel more confident with their speaking ability?

Methods

Participants

Five male students from China were selected from an ESL course for international teaching assistants (ITAs). These ITAs are graduate students who had been offered teaching assistantships, but were not allowed duties involving high levels of interactions with students due to their limited proficiency based on their scores on a test of spoken English. They were, however, allowed to lead recitations or assist with grading. At the end of the semester they were required to be retested to determine if they were proficient enough to teach undergraduate courses. All ten male students (8 Chinese and 2 Koreans) in the class were asked to participate and agreed to take part in the study. The participants were randomly paired with one classmate. The pairs remained the same throughout the five sessions. In one session in which a student was absent, the researcher chatted with the student's partner. Data was gathered for all ten students as they carried out the chat activities. However, data from only five selected students was analyzed. Selection of the participants was based on two factors: (a) Only students from China were selected to eliminate the variable of nationalities, and (b) participants needed to attend all five data gathering sessions.

Tasks

During each of the five fifty-minute sessions, participants completed Task 1, a fifteen-minute communicative task in which they exchanged information about a specific topic with a partner through ICQ chat software. Table 1 presents a summarized description of Task 1 for each of the five sessions. Upon completion, they came together as a class to carry out Task 2. Task 2 for the first three sessions (Sessions 1-3) entailed a report from each student in the class (participants and non-participants) regarding their chat discussion with their partners. No time limit was given but the oral reports spanned between one to three minutes. For the last two sessions (Session 4-5), students participated in an open discussion based on the assigned topic. Students used references from the chats with their partners and responded to statements made by other students during the open discussion.

Table 1. Description of communicative tasks used as the first task for five sessions

SESSION	DESCRIPTION
1	Each partner shared three qualities of a roommate. Then they ranked the six qualities according to their level of importance.
2	Each participant was assigned either the role of a main character or the character's brother. Together, they decided which of their six family members would get the three available life jackets when their boat capsized.
3	Students took on the roles as representatives of ITAs on a student committee to propose a lower tuition hike and present the consequences of a higher tuition hike.
4	Each participant presented either three advantages or disadvantages of the Internet on people's social life and tried to persuade their respective partners to change their minds.
5	Each participant presented their argument whether work experience or paper qualification is more important as a career requirement.

Software and hardware configuration

Ten Intel computers with Windows 95 and Internet access to run the chat software were used for the chat sessions. ICQ, a type of chat software was pre-installed. Unlike other synchronous chat programs such as Daedalus InterChange or Yahoo Instant
Messenger which only allow users to view the final version of their partners' composed discourse, ICQ presents the users with a split screen in which they view their own messages as each letter is typed in the top box as well as each letter in their partners' composed discourse in real time as they are typed in the bottom box. Hence, speakers can choose to co-construct the discourse without having to wait for their partners to send completed phrases or sentences, resulting in a closer resemblance to oral conversation.

Questionnaires

Participants completed two sets of questionnaires, a pre-chat (see Appendix 1) and a post-report questionnaire (See Appendix 2) during each session. These questionnaires were used to indicate the learners' state communicative self-confidence before and after they carried out Tasks 1 and 2. Each questionnaire included twenty-five items that were rated on a 5-point Likert scale ranging from (1) Strongly Agree to (5) Strongly Disagree. Responses for items with negative constructions (e.g. don't, not) were reversed (i.e. 1 is switched to 5 and 2 is switched to 4) before adding the points so that a higher point would reflect a higher level of state communicative self-confidence. For example, Item 3 in the Pre-Chat Questionnaire, *"I am not worried about making mistakes when I talk about this topic in class."* was recoded so that 1 on the Likert scale will be scored as 5 points to indicate a high level of state communicative self-confidence.

To gain content evidence for the validity of the questionnaires, six professors in the TESL/Applied Linguistics program at the university were asked to categorize the twenty-five items from each questionnaire into the three categories: (a) Category A-State Anxiety, (b) Category B-State Self-Perceived Competence, and (c) Category C-Combination of State Anxiety and State Self-Perceived competence.

Procedures

The five sessions, conducted as regular class activities, were carried out over five consecutive Fridays in a research computer laboratory. Students began each session by reading the online instructions for Task 1 followed by verbal instructions to minimize confusion. Instructions for Task 2 were then given to elicit initial responses to Task 2. Next, they completed the pre-chat questionnaire before proceeding with Task 1 for fifteen minutes. Each student used the same computer using pre-established ICQ accounts and worked with the same partner for all five sessions. During Task 2, a microphone and a video camera were used to record the students' oral reports (Sessions 1-3) and open discussions (Sessions 4-5). The video recording served as a backup for the audio recording as well as a means of identifying the participants as they took turns, particularly during the open discussions. No time limit was set, so students spoke as much as they wanted.

After the completion of Task 2, the students completed the post-report questionnaire and wrote a short journal about their experiences during the sessions. Guidelines (Appendix 3) were provided for the first four sessions. Students were instructed to reflect on the whole five sessions during the last session. No guidelines were given, so that they could write anything they felt or recalled at that time.

Analysis

This study refers to both qualitative and quantitative data to answer the two research questions. The number of turns taken in Sessions 4 and 5 compared with the total number of turns indicates the participants' WTC. Since participants are not required to speak unless they wish to, any attempts to take a turn (including unsuccessful attempts) are regarded as an expression of WTC. These attempts are revealed in the video recording. The number of words uttered in Sessions 4 and 5 were also compared with the total number of words. The comparisons, presented in raw scores and percentages, are used to indicate the participants' WTC. High percentages would reflect high WTC.

Consistency in calculation is monitored through pre-established guidelines for determining the number of turns and words. The number of turns is based on the times participants take the floor. Words produced in an uninterrupted stretch constitute a turn. An interruption of another speaker's turn is also considered a turn. If a speaker offers a word or phrase while another speaker is speaking, it is regarded as a turn since the attempt to help reflects WTC. However, laughter is not considered as a turn and a stretch of words that is continued with another stretch of words due to an interruption by laughter is still considered as the same turn.

The number of words is based on complete words uttered by the participants regardless of their accuracy or intended meaning. Words that lacked final consonants or syllables are completed if the speaker's intended words were obvious, and these words are included in the count. In addition, only words produced in stretches of talk longer than one word are counted. Words that are unclear and not transcribed are excluded. Obvious cases of word repetition, for example, *"The Internet discouraged...discouraged youngsters"* are excluded as well. Finally, false starts *("The Internet...In my opinion, youngsters...")* and non lexical pause fillers *("uh" and "um")* are also excluded.

The averaged score of all twenty-five items in the two questionnaires represents the level of state communicative self-confidence. A low averaged score indicates a low level of state communicative self-confidence while a high score indicates a high level of state communicative self-confidence. In addition, a low averaged score for Category A—State Anxiety suggests a high level of state anxiety and vice-versa. On the contrary, a low average score for Category B—State Self-Perceived Competence signifies a low level of state self-perceived competence and vice-versa. The difference[2] between the two averaged scores is used to reveal the overall impact of text chat on the participants' state communicative self-confidence. In addition, the participants' journal entries are included as qualitative data to provide an insight into the participants' responses towards the chat experiences.

Results and discussion

Chat and the willingness to communicate (WTC)

The numbers and percentages of turns taken and words uttered in the open discussion in Sessions 4 and 5 were used to reflect the participants' WTC. These percentages, shown in Table 2, were compared with "Others" which accounted for the number and percentage of turns and words by the remaining five students (four in Session 5 as one non-selected participant was absent).

Table 2. Number and percentage of turns and words in Session 4 and Session 5

---

2. The use of subtracted scores for analysis is based on a qualitative approach. The data from the small sample and short time frame would not have yielded any statistical significance.

Participants	TURNS				WORDS			
	Session 4		Session 5		Session 4		Session 5	
	#	%	#	%	#	%	#	%
1	1	2.33	4	13.33	2	0.14	221	17.89
2	7	16.28	5	16.67	181	13.11	283	22.91
3	10	23.26	8	26.67	307	22.23	295	23.89
4	1	2.33	0	0.00	61	4.42	0	0.00
5	0	0.00	1	3.33	0	0.00	6	0.49
Others	24	55.81	12	40.00	830	60.10	430	34.82
Total	43	100	30	100	1381	100	1235	100

Overall, chat partners, Participants 2 and 3 consistently took more turns and produced more words than the other participants in both sessions while chat partners, Participants 4 and 5 chose not to participate in Session 5 and 4 respectively. Participant 1, on the other hand, took fewer turns in Session 4 compared to Session 5.

The impact of chat on WTC could be either positive or negative, depending on the perception of the learner towards the chat experience. Participant 2, for instance, took more than 16% of the total turns in both sessions. His WTC was higher because he felt more prepared to speak after chatting:

It is a excellent form for us to speak. Because we have already write down the words. We can also easily to speak it out.

Participant 1 also showed a high level of WTC as he took more turns and produced more words in Session 5. He felt more prepared to speak because the chat sessions had helped the organization of his ideas as indicated in his journal entry, *"I think it is good to help organize ideas."* In addition, his experience with technology seemed to be quite positive as he suggested the use of more sophisticated technology as indicated in his journal entry below:

If we speak on the microphone and the word would appear on screen and also we can hear from the partner. That would be great.

Participant 4 and Participant 5 did not display a high level of WTC as they took very little initiative to participate in the open discussion. However, it is interesting to note that Participant 4 indicated in his journal entry that he liked the open discussions the best, but he did not participate much in the sessions. Similarly, Participant 5 said that he had *"many points of view on this topic,"* but he did not choose to share them verbally during the sessions. Since there was evidence of on-task discussion in their chat transcripts, and their journal entries provided no explanation for their reluctance to speak, it was assumed that the chat did not have a positive impact on their WTC.

The results in Table 2 show that the impact of chat on WTC can vary greatly from learner to learner. These results also indicate that the chat experience alone will not necessarily guarantee an increase in WTC. The attitudes of partners seem to play a role in determining the impact of chat as well. For example, Participant 3, who took about a quarter of the total turns in each session, reflected a great deal of enthusiasm in his chat session as seen in his message to his partner in his chat transcript, *"come on, come on, we will fight each other on some hot topic, guy, I do not be afraid of you."* Together with his partner, Participant 2, they contributed approximately 40% of the open discussions in both turns and words. On the other hand, Participants 4 and 5 participated in less than 5% of the open discussion.

It appears that text chats help improve WTC if learners receive adequate constructive input from their partners. If provided with adequate constructive input, learners feel more prepared and organized, and therefore more willing to communicate.

Chat and state communicative self-confidence

In response to the second research question, the averaged score from the pre-chat questionnaire was subtracted from the averaged score of the post-report questionnaire (i.e., Post Report—Pre Chat) and the difference was used to measure the participants' state self-confidence.

Since the time allotted for the chat was so short, the expected difference in the average score was minimal. In the event that a participant has marked "3" on the Likert Scale in the pre-chat questionnaire, his averaged score was 3.00. If he marks a "4" in at least half of the total items in the post-report questionnaire, his averaged score was 3.50, bringing the difference between the questionnaires to a total of 0.50. Therefore, any positive difference higher than 0.50 would be regarded as a positive impact while any negative score higher than -0.50 was regarded as a negative impact.

Table 3. Difference between averaged scores (post report—pre chat)

Participant	Session 1	Session 2	Session 3	Session 4	Session 5
1	0.76	0.96	0.64	0.72	1.00
2	0.20	0.08	0.36	0.00	0.04
3	0.40	0.04	0.28	0.08	0.28
4	-0.56	0.24	-0.16	0.00	-0.68
5	0.52	-0.16	-0.40	-0.40	-0.44

The results in Table 3 show Participant 1 as the only participant who consistently experienced a positive impact. The positive impact was also reflected in his journal entries as he noted *"the chatting part"* as the part of the lesson he liked the most. He also felt *"a little better than before"* and *"more prepared"* after chatting about the topic, and these positive feelings would have increased his state communicative self-confidence.

On the other hand, Participant 4 experienced a negative impact on two occasions, the first and last sessions. His journal entry for Session 1, *"chatting o (sic) not very helpful to our oral English"*, indicated that he did not see how chatting could improve his oral skills. In Session 5, he found the topic to be difficult as indicated in his journal entry, *"the topic on paper qualification and working experience is difficult to discuss."* The irrelevance of the task and difficulty of the topic explained his negative reaction in the two sessions.

A possible reason for the differences in the impact of chat on the participants is the influence of partners. Participants 2 and 3 were chat partners for all five sessions. From their chat transcript, it was evident that they wasted no time on off-task topics and were very involved in their discussions. Therefore, the points that were discussed during the chats were helpful in organizing their ideas and familiarizing them with the required vocabulary, which in turn helped them to be more confident at the time of reporting or participating in the oral discussion. In contrast, Participants 4 and 5 who were partners displayed a more negative reaction to the chat task. In the first session, Participant 5 was more responsive to the chat experience and this response is substantiated by his journal entry, *"I feel it is intresting [sic] and easy to talk with computer."* While this positive response could be due to the novelty of using chat as part of the lesson, his consistent negative response for Sessions 2-5 suggested that there was another factor influencing his state communicative self-confidence. This factor is likely to be the attitude of his partner, Participant 4, who did not see the relevance of text chat in a speaking class. For example, in their chat transcript for Session 2, Participant 4 typed, *"I think this is not a good topic to talk on net…the situation is a lillte [sic] strange."* He often initiated the chat with off-task conversations such as *"listening to mp3"* while his partner tried to keep him on-task. Participant 5 expressed this in his oral report as he said *"My brother doesn't like to talk with this topic and I give him one suggestion, just take it as a hypothesis"* (Oral report 2) and *"So I find three reasons to object so great an increase, and my partner didn't give one"* (Oral report 3). The lack of useful input from his partner would have caused him to rely more on his own opinions. Therefore, he was not able to feel confident while giving his oral report or participating in the open discussion. His state communicative self-confidence continued to decrease as he found the chat to be meaningless and a waste of time.

Chat and state anxiety

Questionnaire items in Category A are averaged and used to measure the participants' state anxiety. Here, the difference between the averaged scores for the post-report questionnaire and the pre-chat questionnaire (Post Report minus Pre Chat) is used to reflect the impact of text chat on state anxiety. Since the scoring for the items has been reversed, a higher score in this category would indicate a lower state anxiety and vice-versa, while a positive score for the difference between the post-report and pre-chat averaged score will indicate a reduction in state anxiety. Like the section before, only results higher than 0.50 or lower than -0.50 will be regarded as a change in state anxiety.

Table 4. Difference in averaged scores for Category A—state anxiety (post report—pre chat)

Participant	Session 1	Session 2	Session 3	Session 4	Session 5
1	0.89	1.11	0.33	0.67	0.67
2	0.22	0.22	-0.22	-0.11	-0.22
3	0.67	-0.22	0.11	0.00	-0.11
4	-0.56	0.11	-0.22	0.00	-0.78
5	0.78	-0.33	-0.22	-1.11	-0.56

The results in Table 4 show similar patterns to the results in Table 3. Participant 1 was again the only one who consistently felt the positive influence of the chat in reducing his state anxiety. Since he felt *"a little better"* and *"more prepared"*, he was less anxious about reporting to his classmates.

Participant 5 in the chat task displayed a positive response only in the first session. His level of state anxiety increased over the subsequent four sessions with the highest negative score of -1.11 for Session 4. As discussed in the previous section, his negative reaction was likely due to the ineffective chat discussion he had with his partner, resulting in a lack of useful input. This was further confirmed by his comment in his fourth journal entry that he had *"many points of view"* on the topic yet chose not to participate at all in the open discussion in Session 4.

Chat and state self-perceived competence

In Table 5, the difference between the averaged scores for Category B for post-report and pre-chat questionnaires was used to analyze the influence of the chat experience on the state self-perceived competence. Like the previous discussion, any scores higher than 0.50 or lower than -0.50 will be regarded as impact of chat on state self-perceived competence.

Table 5. Difference in averaged scores for Category B—state self-perceived competence (post report—pre chat)

Participant	Session 1	Session 2	Session 3	Session 4	Session 5
1	1.38	0.99	1.02	1.55	1.61
2	0.26	0.18	0.93	0.38	-0.25
3	0.75	0.12	0.83	0.52	0.86
4	-0.26	0.67	0.01	0.12	-0.61
5	0.46	-0.19	-0.54	0.07	-0.70

Overall, the results in Table 5 show eleven instances of positive scores (> 0.50) and only three negative scores (< -0.50). The positive scores are also higher than those in Table 4, which indicates that the chat had a more positive impact on state self-perceived competence compared to state anxiety. Participant 1 and Participant 3 believed that the chatting did help them tremendously in their organization and expression of ideas, sentence construction and use of related vocabulary. These beliefs were reflected in their journal entries below.

> *It's [The chat] good to help us develop idea.* (Participant 1, Journal Entry 2)
> *The lesson is good to organize idea.* (Participant 1, Journal Entry 3)
> *I believe it would be better if we have longer time to first disscuss [sic] by ICQ, it*

is constructive. (Participant 3, Journal Entry 1)
I am familiar with those words now, eg tuition fee. (Participant 3, Journal Entry 3)

Conclusion

The analyses of the results reveal that attitudes of partners can influence learners' WTC and state communicative self-confidence. The chat software serves as a medium that can facilitate the preparation process, provided both learners have positive attitudes towards the chat experience. The willingness of the learners to speak after the chat experience is highly dependent on the quality and quantity of input received during the chat experience as revealed by the opposite reactions in the two pairs of chat partners. If one or both partners are extremely enthusiastic and take active roles during the chat session, the levels of WTC and state communicative self-confidence are likely to increase. On the contrary, a negative attitude of a partner in a chat task can influence the perception of the other partner and also cause the partner to feel less prepared to speak since he has not received enough input during the chat. Hence, teachers who plan to use similar chat tasks in the speaking classroom should pair students carefully. They should also consider the attitudes of their students towards technology before choosing to use chat tasks in the speaking classroom.

Topics of discussion can also influence the impact of chat on learners' WTC and state communicative self-confidence. Topics that are more relevant to learners would encourage their interest, while topics that are hypothetical in nature may or may not encourage discussion since the personality of the learners may come into play. If learners like the challenging nature of hypothetical situations, they are likely to engage in the discussion while learners who do not see the relevance of the situation are less likely to participate actively. In addition, the authenticity of the topic has to match the chat situation. For example, the use of chat to negotiate the distribution of life jackets in a hypothetical situation in which a boat is sinking is a mismatch between topic and medium resulting in confusion for some learners. Furthermore, for topics that lend to opposing views, learners should be allowed to select their own position rather than being assigned a position. Learners who are in higher level classes should be given more open-ended topics to stimulate and challenge their thinking abilities.

Learners with low speaking abilities and low state communicative self-confidence will find the chat tasks helpful in lowering their state anxiety and increasing their state self-perceived competence as they will feel more prepared to speak after sorting out their ideas and thoughts, constructing sentences and receiving relevant and useful input from their partners. Therefore, chat tasks may be more beneficial in beginning or lower intermediate classes compared to upper intermediate or advance classes.

Due to the limitations of this study, the findings must be interpreted with caution. Since there are many variables influencing WTC, there should be more careful studies on controlling the variables in order to establish the internal validity of the research. While the results are not conclusive, they provide initial support for the development of more elaborate research on using text chat to improve L2 speaking skills.

The resemblance of chat language to spoken language needs to be further "harnessed" for positive benefits in any ESL/EFL speaking classroom. If learners do perceive the chat language as similar to spoken language, they may be willing to acquire the language through this electronic medium. In addition, chat software supporting voice conversations could be evaluated for their potential benefits in improving L2 speaking abilities.

The results of this study have also shown the use of chat has little impact on reducing language anxiety. Recognizing the established finding of other studies that there is a negative correlation between anxiety and performance, more extensive effort should be made to study other ways of using CALL to minimize language anxiety so that learners will be more willing to seek out opportunities for oral practice.

References

Cheng, Y. (1998). A qualitative inquiry of second language anxiety: Interviews with Taiwanese EFL students. In J. Katchen & Y. Liung (Eds.), *The proceedings of the Seventh International Symposium on English Teaching* (pp.309-320). Taiwan: Crane Publishing.

Cheng, Y., Horwitz, E.K., & Schallert, D.L. (1999). Language anxiety: Differentiating writing and speaking components. *Language Learning, 49*, 417-446.

Chun, D. (1994). Using computer networking to facilitate the acquisition of interactive competence. *System, 22*, 17-31.

Clément, R., Gardner, R., & Smythe, P. (1980). Social and individual factors in second language acquisition. *Canadian Journal of Behavioural Science, 12*, 293-302.

Clément, R., & Kruidenier, B. (1985). Aptitude, attitude and motivation in second language proficiency: A test of Clément's model. *Journal of Language and Social Psychology, 4*, 21-37.

Cohen, Y., & Norst, M. (1989). Fear, dependence, and loss of self-esteem: Affective barriers in second language learning among adults. *RELC Journal, 20*, 61-77.

Daly, J., & Wilson, D. (1983). Writing apprehension, self-esteem, and personality. *Research in the Teaching of English, 17*, 327-341.

DiMatteo, A. (1991). Communication, writing, learning: An anti-instrumentalist view of network writing. *Computers and Composition, 8* (3): 5-19.

Horwitz, E., Horwitz, M., & Cope, J. (1986). Foreign language classroom anxiety. *Modern Language Journal, 70*, 125-132.

Mabrito, M. (1992). Computer-mediated communication and high-apprehensive writers: Rethinking the collaborative process. *The Bulletin* (December): 26-30.

MacIntyre, P., Clément,R., Dörnyei, Z., & Noels, K. (1998). Conceptualizing willingness to communicate in a L2: A situational model of L2 confidence and affiliation. *Modern Language Journal, 82*, 545-563.

MacIntyre, P., & Gardner, R. (1991). Investigating language class anxiety using the focused essay technique. *Modern Language Journal, 75*, 296-304.

MacIntyre, P., Noels, K., & Clément, R. (1997). Biases in self-ratings of second language proficiency: The role of language anxiety. *Language Learning, 47*, 265-287.

Pellettieri, J. (2000). Negotiation in cyberspace: The role of chatting in the development of grammatical competence. In M. Warschauer & R. Kern (Eds), *Network-based language teaching: Concepts and practice* (pp. 59-86). Cambridge: Cambridge University Press.

Price, M. (1991). The subjective experience of foreign language anxiety: Interviews with anxious students. In E. Horwitz & D. Young (Eds.), *Language anxiety: From theory and research to classroom implications* (pp.101-108). New Jersey: Prentice Hall.

Schlenker, B., & Leary, M. (1985). Social anxiety and communication about the self. *Journal of Language and Social Psychology, 4*, 171-192.

Selfe, C. (1990). Technology in the English classroom: Computers through the lens of feminist theory. In C. Handa (Ed.), *Computers and community: Teaching composition in the twenty-first century* (pp.118-139). Portsmouth, NH: Heinemann.

Turbee, L. (1999). Classroom practice: MOO, WOO, and more—Language learning in virtual environments. In J. Egbert, & E. Hanson-Smith (Eds.), *CALL environments: Research, practice and critical issues* (pp. 346-361). Alexandria, VA: TESOL, Inc.

Young, D. (1991). Creating a low-anxiety classroom environment: What does language anxiety Research suggest? *Modern Language Journal, 75*, 426-439.

APPENDIX 1: Pre-CHAT Questionnaire

Directions: Please fill in the information requested below. Your answers will be kept confidential and only the researcher will have access to the information you provide.

Name: _____

Instructions: Circle the number that reflects your opinion for each of the statements.

Scale:

1	2	3	4	5
X	X	X	X	X
Strongly Agree	Agree	Neither Agree nor Disagree	Disagree	Strongly Disagree

#	Statement	1	2	3	4	5
1.	I am not familiar with the vocabulary required for the topic. (B)	1	2	3	4	5
2.	I don't like to talk about this topic because I take too much time to construct my sentence. (C)	1	2	3	4	5
3.	I am not worried about making mistakes when I talk about this topic in class. (A)	1	2	3	4	5
4.	I find it easy to talk about this topic in English. (B)	1	2	3	4	5
5.	I worry that my fluency will prevent my classmates from understanding me. (A)	1	2	3	4	5
6.	I feel self-conscious when I have to talk about this topic. (A)	1	2	3	4	5
7.	I don't feel tense if I have to share my ideas about this topic. (A)	1	2	3	4	5
8.	I find it difficult to express my ideas about the topic in English. (B)	1	2	3	4	5
9.	I feel comfortable talking about this topic in class. (A)	1	2	3	4	5
10.	I know the words required for this topic. (B)	1	2	3	4	5
11.	I am not afraid to express my opinions about this topic in English. (A)	1	2	3	4	5
12.	I am afraid that my classmates cannot understand when I talk about this topic in English. (A)	1	2	3	4	5
13.	I am able to share my opinions about this topic without feeling nervous. (A)	1	2	3	4	5
14.	I don't need to improve my English because my classmates can understand me when I talk about this topic. (B)	1	2	3	4	5
15.	I feel anxious about speaking English in class. (A)	1	2	3	4	5
16.	I won't feel shy if I make mistakes. (A)	1	2	3	4	5
17.	I am worried that my classmates will be impatient with me if I don't speak clearly and fluently. (A)	1	2	3	4	5
18.	I feel nervous about sharing my views with my classmates. (A)	1	2	3	4	5
19.	I think my classmates will understand me easily when I talk about this topic in class. (B)	1	2	3	4	5
20.	I feel embarrassed volunteering my opinions about this topic in class. (A)	1	2	3	4	5
21.	I will start to panic if I have to talk about this topic in English. (A)	1	2	3	4	5
22.	I will speak softly so that my classmates cannot hear my mistakes. (C)	1	2	3	4	5
23.	I think my classmates will not understand me because of my poor speaking ability. (B)	1	2	3	4	5
24.	I feel relaxed about sharing my ideas on this topic. (A)	1	2	3	4	5
25.	I want to share my ideas about this topic with all my classmates. (C)	1	2	3	4	5

(A) State Anxiety, (B) State Self-Perceived Competence, (C) Combination of State Anxiety and State Self-Perceived Competence (These categorizations do not appear on the actual questionnaire.)

APPENDIX 2: Post-REPORT Questionnaire

Directions: Please fill in the information requested below. Your answers will be kept confidential and only the researcher will have access to the information you provide.

Name: _____

Instructions: Circle the number that reflects your opinion for each of the statements.

Scale:

1	2	3	4	5
X	X	X	X	X
Strongly Agree	Agree	Neither Agree nor Disagree	Disagree	Strongly Disagree

1. The chat provided me with some necessary vocabulary during my oral report. (B)	1	2	3	4	5
2. The chat helped me to construct my sentences in a shorter time during my oral report. (B)	1	2	3	4	5
3. My classmates could not understand me when I shared my views during my oral report. (B)	1	2	3	4	5
4. The chat session helped me to express my ideas in English easily during my oral report. (B)	1	2	3	4	5
5. I felt embarrassed during my oral report. (A)	1	2	3	4	5
6. I was not afraid to express my opinions to the whole class during my oral report. (A)	1	2	3	4	5
7. I didn't feel shy when I made mistakes during my oral report. (A)	1	2	3	4	5
8. I felt self-conscious when I was reporting my opinions on this topic to the whole class. (A)	1	2	3	4	5
9. The chat session helped me to make fewer mistakes during my oral report. (B)	1	2	3	4	5
10. I found it difficult to express my ideas on the topic during my oral report. (B)	1	2	3	4	5
11. The chat session helped me to be more comfortable in sharing my ideas during the oral report. (A)	1	2	3	4	5
12. I didn't feel tense when I was sharing my ideas about this topic during my oral report. (A)	1	2	3	4	5
13. The chat session improved my fluency during my oral report. (B)	1	2	3	4	5
14. I felt nervous when I was giving my oral report. (A)	1	2	3	4	5
15. I started to panic when I had to give my oral report. (A)	1	2	3	4	5
16. I spoke softly so that my classmates could not hear my mistakes during my oral report. (C)	1	2	3	4	5
17. I felt relaxed when I was giving my oral report. (A)	1	2	3	4	5
18. I don't need to improve my English because my classmates could understand me during my oral report. (B)	1	2	3	4	5
19. I knew the words required for the topic during my oral report. (B)	1	2	3	4	5
20. I felt comfortable sharing my opinions during my oral report. (A)	1	2	3	4	5
21. I felt anxious when I was sharing my ideas during my oral report. (A)	1	2	3	4	5
22. I was worried because my classmates seemed impatient with me because I didn't speak clearly and fluently. (C)	1	2	3	4	5
23. I think my classmates could not understand me because of my poor speaking ability. (B)	1	2	3	4	5
24. My classmates understood me easily during my oral report. (B)	1	2	3	4	5
25. I wanted to share my ideas about this topic with all my classmates. (C)	1	2	3	4	5

(A) State Anxiety, (B) State Self-Perceived Competence, (C) Combination of State Anxiety and State Self-Perceived Competence (These categorizations do not appear on the actual questionnaire.)

APPENDIX 3: Guidelines for journal entries

Name: _____

1. What was the topic of discussion?

2. Were you familiar with the topic?

3. What did you feel when you were first assigned the topic in class?

4. Were you prepared to talk about the topic in class?

5. How did you feel after you were given time to chat about the topic?

6. What did you think about the chat software?

7. Did you face any problems during this class activity?

8. Were there any advantages or disadvantages to this lesson?

9. Which part of the lesson did you like the most?

10. Which part of the lesson did you dislike the most?

8

Making feedback last: An integrated approach to feedback in language learning

Felicia Zhang

Abstract

In the process of language learning, especially in a formal foreign language environment such as a university Mandarin Chinese (MC) class in Australia, students often feel that they lack the opportunities to check whether they can be understood by a native speaker of the target language. Usually the only feedback a student gets is from their language teachers whom he/she sees for only a few hours a week. This chapter reports on the effect of an experiment that involves the creation of a language learning environment in which physical and technological ways of perceiving MC sounds had been taught to students as a means of providing long lasting feedback in the classroom and/or self-access learning situations. These classes utilized a variety of computer enhanced language tools such as teacher-produced CD-ROMs, and an audio-visual feedback tool (Sptool) (Zhang & Newman, 2003). These speech tools allow the incorporation of a visual representation of student's production that can be compared to the speech of a native speaker. The findings of this study suggest that the experimental group's rate of acquisition of MC pronunciation is faster than other learners who were taught the same course using the romanization system of MC and other traditional load lightening measures. Students in the experimental group also developed better rhythm and stress when speaking Mandarin and were more motivated in their learning.

Introduction

Receiving good quality feedback is an essential aspect of language learning especially at the beginning stages. Feedback is important because it is essential for teaching to be turned into learning and can play a significant role in students' development by providing the knowledge required for improvement (Hinett, 1998; Hyland, 2000). However, in order for the feedback to be effective, two objectives must be met: (1) to enable students to understand feedback and to make sense of it; and (2) to establish a common understanding of how this feedback may be implemented or acted upon by students.

In a language learning classroom error correction, body language, non-verbal behavior, facial expressions, gestures, and tone of voice are all used in communicating feedback. Such feedback is usually instantaneous, involuntary (from the feedback provider), episodic and disappears very quickly from the memory of everyone involved. So in a traditional classroom, while we receive a huge amount of feedback on language production, the feedback received seldom becomes a viable guidance leading to long-term learning in a real, face-to-face communicative interaction outside the classroom.

This chapter reports on the effect of an experiment that involves the creation of a learning environment in which physical and technological ways of perceiving the Mandarin Chinese (MC) sound system had been taught to students as ways of providing long lasting feedback in the classroom and/or self-access learning situations. One of the most important parts of this environment is the use of a speech analysis tool (Sptool) for offering audio and visual feedback. This speech tool allows the incorporation of a visual representation of a student's production that can be easily compared to the speech of a native speaker. Acknowledging that students can seldom make sense of the large amount of feedback offered in the classroom and usually find it very difficult to act upon the feedback received, it is proposed that the specific forms of the feedback obtained through the mechanism of combining physical gestures and Sptool will make the process of understanding the feedback and acting upon it easier and more accessible to students.

This chapter consists of the following sections: (1) a discussion of the theoretical framework that informs the experiment; (2) a discussion of the teaching context and methodology involving the use of the speech tool; (3) a detailed description of the various features of the speech tool; and (4) some preliminary results of a study involving a group of beginning MC students in an Australian university.

Theoretical underpinning of the study

The theoretical framework that informs this research finds its origins in the works of Petar Guberina, a Croatian psycholinguistic and post-modern scholar, who worked on problems of perception with both the hearing impaired and individuals with normal hearing. This framework is known as the verbo-tonal theory of phonetic correction (Renard, 1975). In the context of learning a foreign language, a person with normal hearing in his/her mother tongue will behave as though he/she were hard of hearing. Each language sound carries all frequencies from about 50 Hz to about 16,000 Hz (albeit at various intensities). Theoretically, at any rate, each sound can be heard in many different ways. The ear seems to have a 'choice' as to what to hear in practice depending on the way the ear has been trained. L2 students tend to make 'choices' in the target language based on what they are familiar with in their mother tongue. Troubetzkoy (1969) refers to this as the mother tongue 'sieve'.

Each sound has a particular 'optimal' frequency (i.e. the frequency band, or combination of frequency bands) at which a native-speaker best recognizes and perceives the sound in question according to their mother tongue. Students who experience difficulty with a particular foreign language sound are considered as not having recognized its optimum. Hence, they are unable to reproduce the sound correctly. One of the ways in which students can be made to perceive the optimum of each sound is to remove (e.g. through electronic filtering) any interfering frequencies that might prevent it from being perceived. In this way it is possible, in theory, to by-pass the mother tongue 'sieve' (Troubetzkoy, 1969). Once this has been achieved, students will be able to perceive, for the very first time, the specific quality of the troublesome sound. However, exposing the students to the native speaker optimum may still be insufficient. A set of 'corrective' optimums then needs to be determined. These will be such as to direct a student's audition away from its natural tendency to structure as it has always done.

Verbo-tonalism postulates that the articulation of sounds poses relatively little difficulty once the specific quality of the sound has been heard. Consequently, the determination of corrective OPTIMUMS, for any one student will be established on the basis of his/her pronunciation. It is through exposure to corrective optimals, followed by intensive articulatory practice that students can access valid acoustic models constituting the normal range for the phonemes of language. The course' intense language exposure via a variety of computer assisted tools, including the Sptool, plus the intensive articulatory practice carried out in a 2-

hour lecture provide students with such valid acoustic models of the phonemes of the L2.

Audition is another form of total behavior response to learning that occurs at the whole body level. In this experiment, the steps in the lecture sequence had been designed to integrate phonation and expressiveness which occur in the space between the lungs and the nasal cavity with the breathing, moving, feeling patterns of a person in his/her entirety so that a multitude of memory traces will be retained in different parts of the body.

Given the complexity of the various processes involved in perception and phonation, an intellectualization of these processes is unlikely to be successful. Learning processes must therefore operate at the unconscious level. The fact that translation into English, romanization in Pinyin and tone diacritics (the traditional cognitive load lightening measures) are not emphasized or used at all in this course suggests that the course is especially designed to allow new language to be processed unconsciously first and foremost.

The elements described in the following lecture sequence and the audio-visual materials contained in the teaching materials represent the pedagogic measures that integrate the senses of the body with movement and the process of ear training through working on a system of errors rather than isolated elements of the language. It is proposed that starting an audition process from intonation would result in the proper training of several systems at once in MC. These pedagogic measures also are designed to instil in students certain memory traces by physically 'marking' on their brains so that these memory traces can be reactivated once feedback either from the Sptool or from any other sources has been received.

These memory traces are essential in enabling students to act upon the feedback received. This is another important objective of any feedback system. In this sense, it is essential to gain a clear understanding of what these pedagogic measures are and in what ways they might contribute to the learning and feedback processes.

The teaching context and methodology

Students who studied MC in the first semester, 2003 in a subject called 'Chinese 1A: Language and Culture' at the University of Canberra constituted the experimental group. These students were zero-beginners when they started and were taught exclusively by this whole body learning approach with the use of the Sptool by the researcher and writer of this chapter. The subject materials have been used for a number of years with previous groups and this group of students. Significant differences between this group of students and previous groups were that this group was exclusively taught through a multi-sensory teaching methodology and was the only group who were exposed to the Sptool. In the experimental group, there were 3 students from Japan, 1 student from Korea, 6 Australian students and 1 Australian Chinese student who had minimal exposure to Cantonese. By the end of the experiment, they would have completed 65 contact hours of lectures and tutorial over one semester. Only the Australian students were considered total zero-beginners of MC. Only oral and interview data from the total zero-beginners of MC in this group will be discussed in this chapter. The data from the experimental group of students will be compared with data from previous groups of students using the same subject materials through the same oral and written testing mechanisms.

A new method of teaching MC pronunciation to beginners

The activities in the lecture sequence were all concerned with focusing on the rhythm and intonation of the language. All linguistic items were presented in their situational contexts so that students were engaged in meaningful and useful language practice. The smallest unit of the language being presented is a sentence rather than individual words or compounds. This is because in MC, the acoustic characteristics of the words change when they are in a sentential environment. For instance, when a word is read in isolation, the frequency of the word is different from when the word is part of a sentence (Jinfu, 1991:247; Kratochvil, 1998). So concentrating one's effort in mastering the citation form of the tones of individual words or compounds does not guarantee success in producing the sentences containing those words.

The lecture sequence consists of the following steps:
Step 1: the imagery of the 'little white cloud' was used to relax the students and the teacher. This constitutes the 'relaxation phase'. This sets up a relaxed atmosphere for learning for the rest of the lesson. As Murdock (1987) points out visualization can facilitate the interiorisation of knowledge by creating a more receptive state of awareness, permitting the affective and creative functions of a more holistic nature to participate in and strengthen the learning experience.

Step 2: Students and the teacher walk around in circles and hum along to the rhythm of the sentences without vowels and consonants (5 times). This is used to highlight the intonation and rhythm of MC. Ideally, this step should be accompanied by the filtered version of the target sentence. The filtered version of the sentences is produced by filtering out sounds that are above 320 Hz in the sound spectrum. However, without suitable equipment such as extremely loud speakers with a heavy base sound, listening to the filtered version is extremely uncomfortable for students. The humming in the lecture sequence takes the place of the filtered version and is more readily accessible.

Step 3: Students and the teacher clap to the rhythm and the beat of the language. This allows students to experience the rhythm of the sentence and observe different groupings of the words in a sentence. It also allows the students to observe how stress, realized by length and loudness in MC, is tied to meaning. This also enables them to observe the key words in a sentence and realize that not all words are of equal value and that in making oneself understood, one only needs to get the key words right to be understood. This training is essential in training them the strategy of prediction and advanced planning in listening comprehension.

Step 4: Students and the teacher walk about with feet coming down on every syllable, to get the body used to producing a tense downward tone that is also loud (the 4th tone). Raising or stretching upwards as though attempting to touch the ceiling allows students to experience the tenseness of the body in producing the first high level tone (the 1st tone). Students are also instructed to adopt a forward lumping of the shoulders for the 2nd and 3rd tones in MC as the production of these tones need a relaxed posture.

Research shows that Chinese speakers have a much wider voice range when speaking MC than English speakers speaking English (Chen, 1974). As the first tone (1st tone) starts at a higher frequency than what most Australian speakers are used to, extra physical efforts need to be made to remind one that one must start high. To stretch one's muscular system to express these MC tones, one must not slouch in seats. By asking students to stand up straight and walk in a circle with various gestures, students are experiencing the coordination and synchronization of various muscles with the sounds uttered.

The rest of the lecture was involved in activities that further highlighted the melody of the sentences involved. Throughout the learning sequence, translation and writing down the sentences are not needed until the last moment. By the time students come to write down the meaning, they will have already internalized and memorized the melody of the sentences.

The activities in the lecture sequence offer students a range of physical ways for remembering tones and the rhythm of the language beyond the set contact hours every week. These measures set up a series of learning steps that can be used for self-access learning at home.

The role of the Sptool and the course data CD and audio CD

Course data CD:

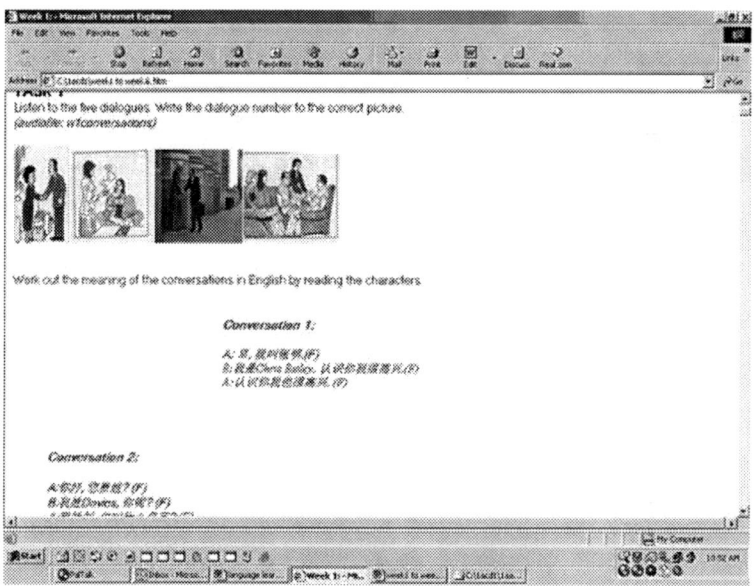

Figure 1 Picture of the teaching material

Each new vocabulary item, new sentence or phrase in the teaching materials is linked to a sound file. These items are indicated in blue. The course data CD also contains teaching materials in html format; all the associated sound files, the speech tool (Sptool) and short video skits through which students can test out their comprehension of the new language learned. An audio CD of the sound files is also provided with the course materials. In 2003, a weekly compulsory class using computer enhanced teaching materials was also arranged.

The role of the Sptool

The Sptool has been designed to provide audio-visual feedback for students' tones and intonation in MC. Many Computer Assisted Pronunciation Technology (CAPT) systems on the market already provide instantaneous feedback in the form of spectrograms and waveforms which are often accompanied for comparison—by previously stored displays of a model utterance pronounced by the teacher or by a native speaker. These systems make use of tools that perform acoustic analyses of amplitude, pitch, duration and spectrum of students' speech. However, according to Neri, Cucchiarini and Strik (2002), two main reasons make these CAPT systems ineffective. First of all, the simultaneous display of the incoming learner's utterance and the model utterance wrongly suggests that the student should ultimately aim at producing an utterance whose acoustic representation closely corresponds to that of the model. In fact, even though two utterances have very different waveforms, they may both be very well pronounced according to a native speaker. Secondly, these kinds of displays are not easily interpreted by students, because they provide too much information on the student speech's amplitude, pitch, duration and spectrum, which inhibits the learners from being enable to pick up the most salient aspects of the acoustic signal. Furthermore, CAPT systems such as Winpitch (Martin, 2003) and PRAAT (Boersma & Weenink, 2003) are too hard for students use, if they are not highly computer literate.

Bearing in mind that the feedback provided has to be interpretable and easy-to-use for students, the design of the Sptool is to measure the pitch curves of MC sentences only with the important correlates of MC speech indicated. This means the Sptool is capable of showing the pitch curves as well as length and loudness (correlates of MC) of utterances in MC speech through the display of the height and the length of the words within utterances. The height and length of the curves also correspond to the articulatory gestures needed to produce these tones in the lecture sequence. Combined with the articulatory gestures it is hypothesized that this will make the feedback long lasting. In other words, students will be able to convert the feedback into learning and use it as guidance in real face-to-face communication.

All the written teaching materials were linked to sound files and passed through the Sptool. Once passed through the Sptool, the learner can listen to the teacher's model pronunciation by clicking on the 'teacher' icon. With one click, he/she can hear the model sentence and see the pitch curve of the model sentence displayed on the screen. If the learner wants to hear a smaller chunk of the sen-

Making feedback last: An integrated approach to feedback in language learning   153

tence, then he/she can select the bit of the curve by dragging the cursor over the portion he/she wants to hear. After listening to the sentence numerous times, the learner can decide whether he/she wants to record his/her own production.

Some of the activities in the lecture sequence can be duplicated in different forms through the use of the Sptool. While the classroom sequence is more or less teacher driven and physical, the Sptool allows the lecture sequence to be experienced differently. In the following sample sentence, 'ni3 shi4 cong2 nar3 lai2 de?'

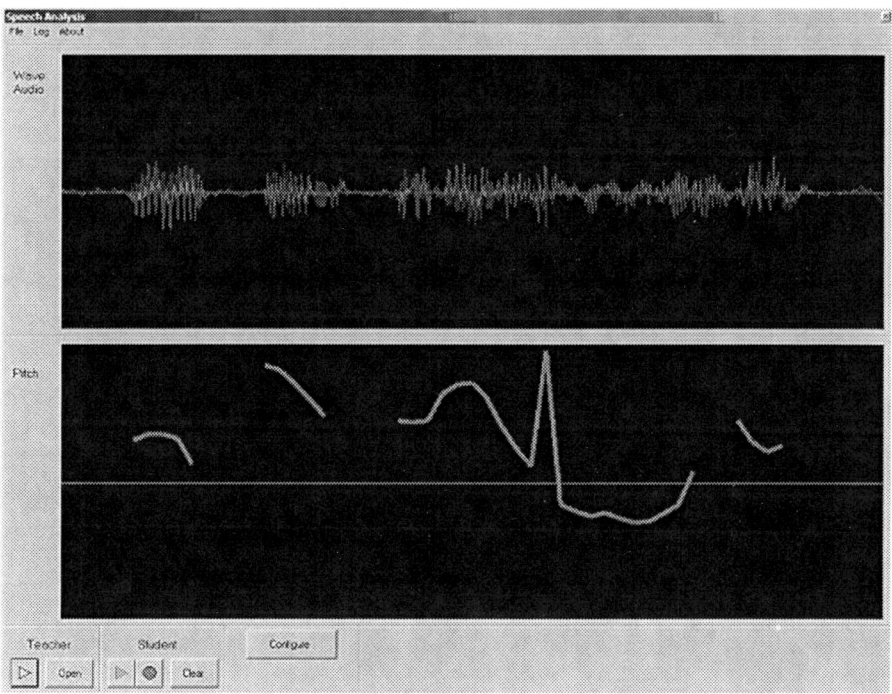

Figure 2 Picture of the Sptool showing the sample sentence: Where are you from? (ni3 shi4 cong2 nar3 lai2 de0?)

Key

The number following the romanization such 'ni3' refers to the tones in MC. '1' refers to the 1st high level tone; '2' refers to the 2nd tone; '3' refers to the 3rd tone; and '4' refers to the 4th tone.

'cong2 nar3 lai2' is a key string of words and the curve clearly shows that the four characters are in a group together and are being stressed and is longer in duration. This information is extremely important when training students to accept that the ultimate aim of producing a utterance which is acceptable by native speakers is NOT to produce an utterance whose acoustic representation is an exact match or even closely corresponds to that of the model. It is vital to impress upon the students that the importance in producing a comprehensible sentence in MC is to be able to produce the **key parts** of the utterance correctly.

The following visual curve shows the sentence 'Nin2 gui4xing4?'

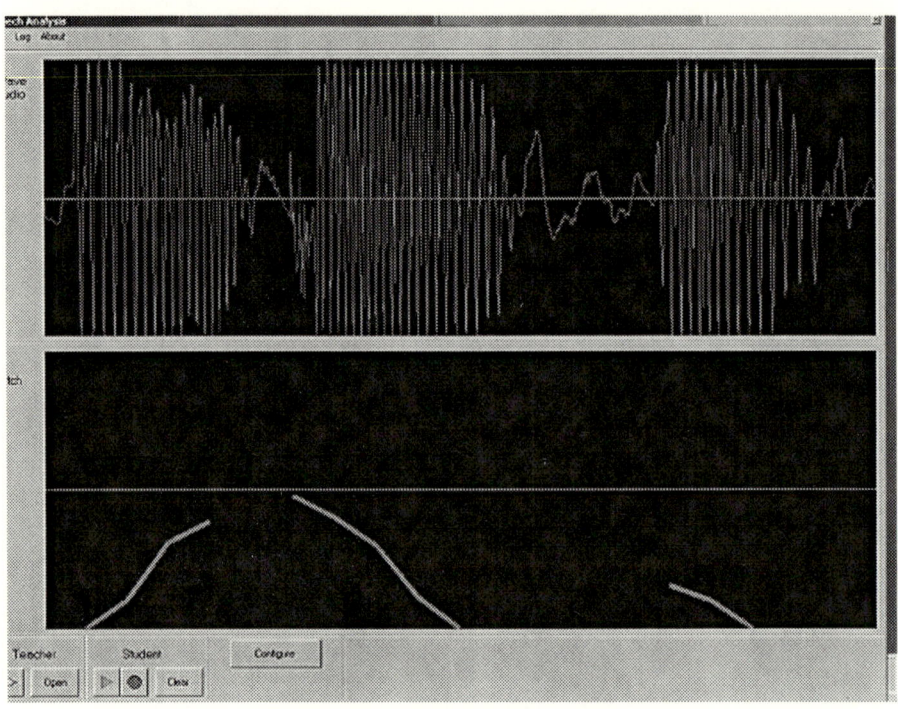

Figure 3 Picture of the Sptool showing the sample sentence: What is your honorable surname? (Nin2 gui4 xing4?)

In the sentence 'Nin2 gui4 xing4?' (What is your honorable surname?) though both 'gui4' and 'xing4' are in fourth tones on paper, clearly, the stress on them are different with 'gui4' being emphasized more. Through repeated listening and copying, students not only can be guided by the curves, they can also get a sense of what is being stressed and what is not.

The height (related to the muscular tenseness of the body) of both first and fourth tones in MC (e.g. gui4 in the previous example) is also indicated clearly with respect to other tones. The height of the first and fourth tones reminds the students of the need to stretch their voice range beyond their normal voice range. This information is very useful in enabling students to change their way of producing the target sentences after observing the differences between the native speaker's production and theirs.

The use of the Sptool encourages students to reflect on and explore in the process of learning. Many of the explorations cannot be pre-determined or even imaged by a teacher. In this experiment, many of the tasks that were done were initiated by the students through use. Furthermore, being able to experience each sentence repeatedly through the Sptool creates an environment in which students can totally immerse themselves consciously and unconsciously in the language.

The study

Participants

Three groups of beginners of Mandarin Chinese were involved. The first group ('group 1') consists of total beginning Australian students from 1995 and 1996 who were taught pinyin (the Chinese romanization) from the beginning of their MC study. The oral test data collected from this group represents the baseline data. This group is referred to as the 'pinyin' group.

The second group ('group 2') finished their two semesters of study in Mandarin in 2001. These participants were zero beginning Australian students enrolled in Chinese 1a: Language and Culture in 2001. By the end of the experiment, they had completed 65 contact hours of lectures and tutorials over one semester. The third group ('group 3') consisted of Australian students who studied MC in the first semester, 2003. This constitutes the experimental group. These students were zero-beginners when they started and were taught exclusively by this multi-sensory methodology with the use of the Sptool. By the end of the experiment, they would have completed 65 contact hours of lectures and tutorials over one semester. Only 6 Australian students were considered total zero-beginners of MC at the beginning of the course. Both group 2 and 3 students had been categorized as the non-pinyin groups in this study. These students were not taught through the use of pinyin at all.

Data collection methods

All three groups of students were tested using a combination of oral tests and written tests. However, due to the lack of space in this chapter, discussion of results will be primarily based up oral data collected from the three groups as well the face-to-face interview data, with the researcher who was also the lecturer for the subject, collected from students in the 2003 group at the end of the first semester in 2003.

Quantitative data

A previous study conducted by the researcher showed that the non-pinyin group of students (based on data collected from Group 2) tended to have a faster rate of Chinese consonant acquisition (Zhang, 2002).

The 1st oral performances (performed after 30 hours of face-to-face teaching) of the students in the 2003 group of students were analyzed. Out of 1827 words (MC characters) uttered, 77 errors were made with consonants and vowels. In other words, only 4.2% of errors were made. Out of the 77 errors, students from non-Australian background made all the errors. The 6 Australian students in Group 3 did not make any consonant errors at all. The results of this study reinforced previous research findings that non-pinyin group of students (Group 2) tended not make any errors with palatals [xi] and [ji] and [qi] at all (Zhang, 2002). Furthermore, the speed of acquisition of MC consonants by Group 3 students was almost twice as fast as that of Group 2 students. After only 30 hours of face-to-face instruction, all the Australian students in Group 3 gained complete control of the initials of MC.

The faster rate of Mandarin sound system acquisition can be attributed to the removal of romanization, the availability of sound files on CDs and the speech tool as well as the physical lecture sequence. The combined effect of these tools appeared to have helped to reduce the transfer effect from the students' mother tongue-English. A close examination of the audio recordings of Group 3 students' oral also suggests that Group 3 students were more fluent and spoke in longer utterances than the students in the previous groups. Though they still had tone problems, the rhythm of their speech was much more natural when compared with a native speaker's rhythm. However, due to the limitation of space in this chapter, the qualitative results obtained from 2003 group of students through the one on one interviews conducted at the end of the first semester will be discussed next.

Qualitative data

The interview data of the students from the 2003 group yielded many interesting specific findings: Two main areas of interests emerged from the interview data. Firstly, it concerns the different ways students made use of the teaching materials provided. Secondly, students were overwhelmingly in support of the two distinctive techniques used in the course: the use of physical movements and gestures in the teaching of MC intonation and the decision not to use pinyin (Chinese romanization system).

Students' different uses of the teaching materials

The sequencing of the materials in the subject is conceived and designed based upon the principle of exploration (from the teacher's/writer's point of view) through listening and speaking rather than reading and writing. Contrary to the teacher's expectation, students tended to focus on reading and writing and then listening and speaking.

There were 3 Japanese students, 1 Korean student, 1 student with a Cantonese background and 6 Australians who are genuinely zero beginners in the class in 2003. I categorized the 3 Japanese, 1 Korean and 1 Cantonese background students into the character-based language group and the rest into the Australian learners group.

In general, students from the character-based language group behaved very differently from the Australian learners who were zero beginners. While the Australian group spent on average 10 hours per week on the subject, the character-based language group student actually only spent on average 2 hours per week on the subject. Similarly, while every Australian student teamed up with a native speaking tutor outside class, the character-based group did not have tutors at all. Furthermore, even though the character-based group of students consisted of all experienced language learners having learned English as a second language, they still basically depended on the printed textbook for learning.

All the students involved tended to start the learning process week by week from working on the characters covered each week on their own. The following are some accounts of how the students utilize their time outside class:

> From the Australian student group (Group 3):
> ……I have been working on the characters, I make up cards and test myself with cards and go over the weeks materials. I found that fairly easy……It (data and audio CD:my clarification)is not a tool I'm used to using. I have

been away from school for10 years now, I am more of a traditional learner, with books and following the course through a textbook and so on but I found them useful, it has been great.

The first thing I will do is I will learn all the characters for that week, I'll do that by making up flashcards and then learning about 5 characters at the time. And just revising them and then using those flash cards to check that I do know them and then build up to 10 characters and 15 characters until I know them all. Once I know all the characters and can recognize them, I start putting them to what they actually sound like and say and then go through the week's work.

The use of the data and audio CD

The character-based language students tended not to use the data CD and used the audio CD only. The Australian students, however, made a lot more use of both CDs.

> From the Australian student group (Group 3):
> The second half of the semester I have really started to take advantage of the Audio CD in my car and the Data CD at home. I am using them more and more now….I somewhat undervalued them. It is not a tool I'm used to using…..The big difference is especially for the language is being able to see something and make the sound for yourself, and then click on the character and have it speak to you and you can check it. I found the audio CD in the car has been great, because that is so much time that has been wasted in the past. And that is good learning time.

> Well, I have had to use all the characters from the CDs and then I transfer them all into word documents and enlarge them. That is how I made the flash cards. But I use mainly the audio section of the CD's, more than anything….It's more the audio files on the data CD because I am using the vocabulary on that and that way I can visualize both of them. I intend to use the audio CD in the car.

Students from both groups were extremely enthusiastic towards the physical activities used in the lecture sequence.

> From the Australian student group (Group 3):
> I found I was actually remembering how we did all the movements and the intonation, I found I could actually recall them……I would like to see more

activities and more interaction in class and now that we have presumably, got the skills now to sort of take home and to sort of self teach a lot of the characters and the tones, it would be much more valuable to use the in class time more interactively.

The cloud is helping, because after you work for 8 hours, it is a lot of work Chinese, just to have a break for 5 min. is good just to clear your mind……Definitely the group work in a circle, clapping, stamping, repeating sentences over and over again is the most useful, more useful than going through the vocabulary. Because it does not give you real practice. And that is what you need: the repetition, and I think that that is the only way you can learn. The first 6 weeks were so good. When it comes to names and ages, we can say them whereas the second part, there was not so much of that, because we had been going through the vocabulary, I found it more difficult….And also, I go home from Chinese and we have been practicing these things in a group circle and stamping, and I'll go home and do it home as well: And I remember it through the day and even at work I do it, people laugh but….When I am doing the actions? Absolutely, definitely, at this stage, I am still doing: Wo hen gaoxing, but now that is so natural, I do not need to put up my hands in the air.

It sort of made the tones physical. Because you are stamping your feet for 4th tone and sort of raising your body for second tones, things like that. You sort of get imagery in terms of physical, what tones represented what.

Students from the character-based language group also found the classroom procedure very useful because it did not rely on any particular computer technology.

I think that it is quite good, after so many times, sometimes I try to remember a new word and then I forget the previous ones, but still something is left in my mind. So sometimes I hear a word and I remember it, unconsciously. Sometimes when I try to explain something to my Chinese friends I would use gestures.

It's like if I stand and walking around, if I walking around using the body, I can remember easily. But just sit down, just listening, it does not help me. If I walk around, I will remember better and easier.

When we are walking we can't write anything so we have to use our memory. I find it is o.k. it's good.

Some students did not actively participate in the physical part of the lecture as they felt that this method of learning is contrary to their usual way of learning. But these students still benefited greatly from pure observation. As one such student from the Australian learners group commented:

> I think that perhaps your emphasis on the tone and not focusing on the pinyin has helped me with the characters. I think it is painful to go through, to not have pinyin. But I think that in the end you start to associate the sound with the character which I think is better and also the tones, the focus on the tones is good, because if you do not have tones, you are not speaking Chinese….but I do know that if I'd pick up a Lonely Planet guide now, for example and I was reading it to my friend, just the knowledge that I have now on tones, I can make it intelligible for her who is speaking Chinese whereas before, when I was reading it, even if you are reading it and you do not know anything about tones, they do not know what you are saying at all. So I think it has worked.

Student's reaction to the Sptool

Sptool only became fully functional after the 6th week of the first semester in 2003, consequently not many students made use of it. However, one student from the Australian learners group consistently used the program and this was how she (student X) described her use of the tool:

> I listen to the teacher probably about 3 times And then I'll say it with the teacher 3 or 4 times and then I record myself and look at the graphs and depending on how close they are, which you can get a pretty good idea of whether you are close or not, I will listen to the teacher again and then I listen to my self again just to see how Chinese I am sounding…I listen perhaps to the length of a sound and I can see the curve, and if I am missing that when I have recorded myself and I go back and I sort of have a look on the curve where it is quite different, you know where it is a lot longer, then I'll go back and listen to that exactly character and see whether it is shi or she.

Even though only one student consistently used the Sptool, 3 other students requested more extensive training in using the tool and suggested that the tool should be introduced right from the beginning of the subject.

Students' reaction to not using pinyin

The romanization system for MC-pinyin—is usually supplied to beginning students in an attempt to make the process of learning MC easier. However, due to the need to eliminate any intellectualization in the audition process, in this particular study, pinyin and tone diacritics were not provided in the teaching materials. Even though the Australian students in the course admitted that the elimination of pinyin made learning more difficult, they also commented that in the long run they learned to analyze each character stroke, recognize radicals and consequently made the learning of the characters easier.

Pedagogical implications

This study examines how classroom physical procedures and the use of the Sptool to receive feedback had been integrated to ensure that feedback has a long lasting effect on students. Due to the delayed release of the Sptool to the students, only one student managed to regularly use the tool. However, the description of how this one student (student X) used the Sptool suggested that the feedback information provided by the tool is not difficult to interpret and the fact that the student could listen to the master recording and then her recording and compared them easily through both listening and visual interpretation. This makes the Sptool very useful in private study. As duration (length of sounds) and amplitude (loudness of the sounds) are important cues to tone identification (Kratochvil, 1984), not just the fundamental frequency of a person's voice, the fact the student X used the length of the curve to guide her suggests that the tool was also capable of guiding her how to physically change her pronunciation as well.

However, the most influential measure to modify students' learning cycle seemed to be the use of physical gestures, walking around and clapping in class. Many students did not only use these measures within the classroom, they utilized them outside class in private study and in real communication. In fact, it is conceivable that these procedures would also help them in interpreting the visual curves provided by the Sptool as well. According to the video tapes of oral performances collected at the end of second semester in 2003, many Australian students from Group 3, the experimental group, actually unconsciously used the gestures to keep the rhythm of their speech going in their oral performances. They were unaware of the fact that they were using the gestures during their performance and realized only what they were doing after being told by the teacher after the performance.

The interview data however, has sounded one caution: as curriculum designers, we must not expect one piece of software or computer technology to do everything. As the findings showed, no matter how we try to design the best software, there will be people who would not have access to use the software and students would always do what they feel is most comfortable rather than follow the route we carve out for them. So in creating an effective learning environment, we need to include a large number of 'machines' they can use for learning rather than expecting one 'machine' to do everything. Finally, we must not forget that learning a language involves physical and psychological transformations, so to expect computer technology to do everything is contrary to the aim of catering for the needs of learners. As one older Asian student put it, "I do not use much of the materials which you provide, like the Data CD, I do not use them, I am not a person who is familiar with machines, I prefer to speak Chinese, and actually get a real reaction from them, that is a better way for me."

The interview and the questionnaire data demonstrated that the Australian students were highly motivated spending up to 10 outside hours on Chinese. Indeed a lot of this enthusiasm and motivation came from having thoroughly enjoyed the innovative procedures used during the lecture segment. So the Sptool had to compete with the physical activities for students' attention and time. In order to really convince the student body the efficacy of the Sptool, the whole learning process can be further improved by:

- having longer and regular training sessions with the use of the Sptool and other computer technology for students;

- using the Sptool also to 'assess' students' production and then share the results with the students;

- linking student feedback to 'feed forward' process. In other words, having frequent discussions of what the tool can be used for with the students can help students in correctly interpret the feedback provided by the tool.

- using the Sptool not just to provide individual feedback to students in the private setting.

It can also be used to provide progressive feedback on their production between peers and between them and their private tutors.

Conclusion

A number of benefits for students related to the general use of technology have been demonstrated in this chapter. In this multi-sensory learning environment, students appeared to gain confidence in directing their own learning. One conclusion one can draw from the data collected is that this learning environment has accomplished one of the hardest tasks in teaching pronunciation of any language, i.e. to facilitate the carryover of teaching points in class into everyday communication.

One significant consideration of creating this environment is the fact that the technology chosen is of a 'low tech' nature utilizing mainly CD-ROM technology. However, even low tech technology cannot solve the problem of the digital divide. Therefore, in constructing a viable and genuinely student-centred learning environment, other alternatives need to be included to ensure that students who do not have access to technology are also adequately catered for.

Another significant finding is that the modular nature of various 'machines' (Deleuze & Guattari, 1987) in this environment has proven to be extremely efficient. The 'machines' used in the environment were easily accessible and user friendly and adaptable. The non-technology driven elements such as one's body, voice, movement and gesture were already available to every student. The technological elements such as the sound, video, text files and the filtered sound files were not hard to produce. The frequency of interaction and ease of access afforded by the Sptool and other sound files had been extremely motivating for students. Through the use of various machines in this multi-sensory environment, feedback, offered through physical and technological means, had acted in concert to greatly motivate students and convert feedback into learning.

References

Boersma, P. A., & Weenink, D. (2003). *Praat* [Speech Analysis]. Institute of Phonetic Sciences University of Amsterdam: Institute of Phonetic Sciences University of Amsterdam.

Chen, G. T. (1974). The pitch range of English and Chinese speakers. *Journal of Chinese Linguistics, 2*(2), 159-171.

Deleuze, G., & Guattari, F. (1987). *A thousand plateaus: Capitalism and Schizophrenia* (B. Massumi, Trans.). Minneapolis,London: University of Minneapolis Press.

Hinett, K. (1998). *The role of dialogue and self assessment in improving student learning.* Paper presented at the British Educational Research Association Annual Conference, The Queen's University of Belfast.

Hyland, F. (2000). ESL writers and feedback: giving more autonomy to students. *Language Teaching Research, 4*(1), 33-54.

Jinfu, G. (1991). Exploration in the tones and intonation of Mandarin Chinese. Beijing Language Institute. [in Chinese].

Kratochvil, C. (1984). Tone and Stress Discrimination in Normal Beijing Dialect Speech. In B. Hong (Ed.), *New Papers on Chinese Language Use* (pp. 119-132.). Canberra: Contemporary China Centre, Research School of Pacific Studies, Australian National University.

Kratochvil, P. (1998). Intonation in Beijing Chinese. In D. Hirst & A. D. C. (Eds.), *Intonation Systems: A Survey of Twenty Languages* (pp. 417-431). Cambridge: Cambridge University Press.

Martin, P. (2003). *Winpitch* (Version 1) [Speech Analysis Tool]: Pitch Instruments.

Murdock, M. (1987). *Spinning inward.* Boston: Shambhala.

Neri, A., Cucchiarini, C., & Strik, H. (2002). *Feedback in computer assisted pronunciation training: Technology push or demand pull?* Paper presented at the Proceedings of ICSLP 2002, Denver, USA.

Renard, R. (1975). *Introduction to the verbo-tonal method of phonetic correction* (B. Morris, Trans.): Didier.

Troubetzkoy, N. S. (1969). *Principles of phonology (Grundzuge de phonologie, travaux du cercle linguistique de prague.)* (C. A. M. Baltaxe, Trans.): University of California Press.

Zhang, F. (2002). *Implementing computer technology into the language learning process: What difference does it make?* Paper presented at the International conference on Computers in Education, Auckland, New Zealand.

Zhang, F., & Newman, D. (2003). *Speech Tool* [Software]. Canberra, Australia: University of Canberra, Australia.

9

Different learners and different feedback: Development of a computer-based essay marking system for ESL learners in Malaysia

Saadiyah Darus, Supyan Hussin and Siti Hamin Stapa

Abstract

Different group of learners require different types of feedback depending on the objectives and types of learning as well as their level of education. It is said that the ideal person to mark learners' work is the instructor of the course. With the advancement of information technology (IT), computer-based essay marking (CBEM) systems have been developed in order to reduce the workload of human markers. Although there have been reports indicating the success in the deployment of CBEM systems in the USA, many lecturers in Malaysia are still not convinced to use these systems in their classrooms. They claimed that these systems lacked human touch and would not be able to give proper evaluation of Malaysian students' essays in English as a second language (ESL). Three studies were conducted to investigate this claim. In the process of carrying out this research, the authors examined users' expectations of a CBEM system and the use of a CBEM system in assessing students' essays at tertiary level of education. The results so far suggest that in order for a CBEM system to be useful to the Malaysian environment, we need to develop a system of our own by taking into account our users' needs and expectations.

Introduction

Some of the roles of marking or grading as it is called in the U.S. are to assess learners' achievement and provide feedback to learners (Walvoord & Anderson, 1998). The aim of giving feedback is to help learners improve their learning ability. Normally, a human marker does the marking and he or she is someone who is closely related to the learners' process of learning. It is said that the ideal person to mark learners' work is the instructor of the course since he or she is the closest person that is able to inform learners of their progress and development in relation to their learning.

Instructors are expected to give feedback on learners' progress since feedback is an essential part of instruction (Mory, 1996; Smith & Ragan, 1992). Feedback given to students closes the loop in a learning process (Gagne, 1985). At the same time, lecturers are also fully aware that different groups of learners require different types of feedback depending on the objectives and types of learning as well as their level of education (Ashwell, 2000; Ferris & Roberts, 2001; Ley, 1999). In so far as writing assessment is concerned,

> The educational purpose of responding to and evaluating writing ought to be the same as the purpose of the writing class: to improve student writing...we have one overriding goal: the students need to see what works and what does not work in the draft, so that revision can take place (White, 1998, p.104).

Silva (1990) noted that second language (L2) writing at least in the U.S., involves the following elements: the L2 writer, the L1 reader, the L2 text, the contexts for L2 writing and the interaction of these elements in a variety of authentic English as a Second Language (ESL) settings.

With the advancement of information technology (IT), computer-based essay marking (CBEM) systems have been developed in order to reduce the workload of human markers in marking students' writing. CBEM systems can be categorized into automated and semi-automated systems (Darus, Stapa, Hussin & Koo, 2000). The most popular automated marking systems are *E-rater* (Burstein & Chodorow, 1999), *Criterion Online Essay Evaluation* (Burstein, Leacock & Chodorow, 2003), *Project Essay Grader* (Page, 1996; Page & Peterson, 1995; Page & Truman, 1994) and *Intelligent Essay Assessor* (Foltz, Laham & Landauer, 1999; Wolfe et al., 1998). *Methodical Assessment of Reports by Computer* (Marshall & Barron, 1987) and *Markin* (Holmes, 1996; Krajka, 2002) are semi-automated marking systems.

Although there have been reports indicating the success in the deployment of some of these CBEM systems in the U.S. (Burstein & Chodorow, 2002; Burstein et al., 1998; Burstein, Wolff & Lu, 1999; Foltz, Kintsch & Landauer, 1998; Shermis, Mzumara, Olson & Harrington, 2001), many lecturers in Malaysia are still not convinced to use these systems in their classrooms. They claimed that these systems lack human touch and would not be able to give proper evaluation of Malaysian students' essays in ESL.

The aim of this chapter is to report progress that had taken place in investigating this claim. In the process of carrying out three studies, Study 1 explored lecturers' expectations of a CBEM system, Study 2 investigated students' expectations of a CBEM system and in Study 3, we experimented the use of a CBEM system in assessing students' essays at tertiary level of education. We will discuss these aspects in turn in the following sections.

Study 1: Investigating lecturers' expectations of a CBEM system

The aim of Study 1 was to investigate the reasons why Malaysian lecturers' at higher learning institutions did not utilize currently available CBEM systems. The study addressed the following research questions:

1. Were the lecturers aware of the availability of these CBEM systems? To answer this question, the study examined the extent at which lecturers have heard and used a CBEM system.

2. What were the lecturers' opinions about a CBEM system? To answer research question 2, this study examined whether the lecturers believe that it is possible for computers to mark essays effectively and whether it will be beneficial to them if the computers can be used to mark essays.

3. What were the expected features that lecturers look for in a CBEM system? To answer research question 3, the study examined desirable functions that a CBEM system should provide.

Methodology

A survey in the form of a questionnaire was developed and distributed to lecturers in the form of e-mail. Some of these lecturers were currently teaching at Universiti Kebangsaan Malaysia and were selected from the university's handbook and homepage. These lecturers gave written assignments to students and could be contacted through e-mails. A total number of 80 respondents participated in this study and the data collected were then analyzed using *Microsoft Excel*.

The questionnaire consisted of 18 questions that were divided into three sections. The first section was about the respondents' background. The second section enquired about their approach to teaching courses and the final section focused on their opinions about a CBEM system.

Background of respondents

Out of 80 lecturers who participated in this study, 52 were female (65%) and 28 were male lecturers (35%). In terms of area of specialization, 22 lecturers specialized in teaching English for economics and business (27.5%), 26 lecturers in teaching English for arts and social science (32.5%) while 40 lecturers (50%) specialized in teaching English in language and education.

Results and discussion

In analyzing their approach to teaching courses, it was gathered that they usually mark the following essay traits: creativity, style, organization of ideas, knowledge or topic content and syntax. The number of lecturers who marked these traits is shown in Figure 1. From this figure, it is clear that 74 lecturers (92.5%) marked organization of students' ideas in essays. 70 lecturers (87.5%) marked knowledge or topic content of an essay. 52 lecturers (65.0%) marked creativity and 42 lecturers (52.5%) marked style. Only 38 lecturers (47.5%) marked syntax.

The findings indicate that the lecturers paid most particular attention to students' organization of ideas. The next important trait that they marked was knowledge or topic content, followed by creativity and style. The trait that had the least importance was syntax.

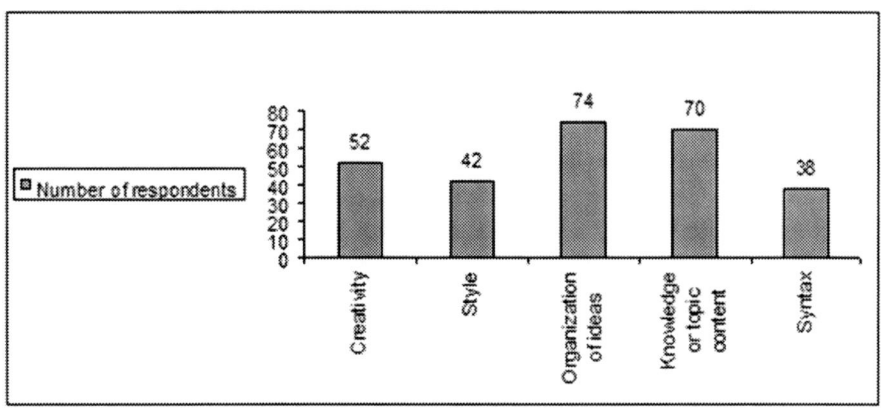

Figure 1 Essay traits that lecturers mark

Figure 2 shows the type of scoring procedure that lecturers used in marking essays. The most common scoring procedure used by the lecturers was holistic scoring, where 58 lecturers (72.5%) used it. The next popular scoring procedure was analytic scoring that was being used by 46 lecturers (57.5%). 20 lecturers (25.0%) used primary trait scoring while 6 lecturers (7.5%) did not use any of these three scoring procedures.

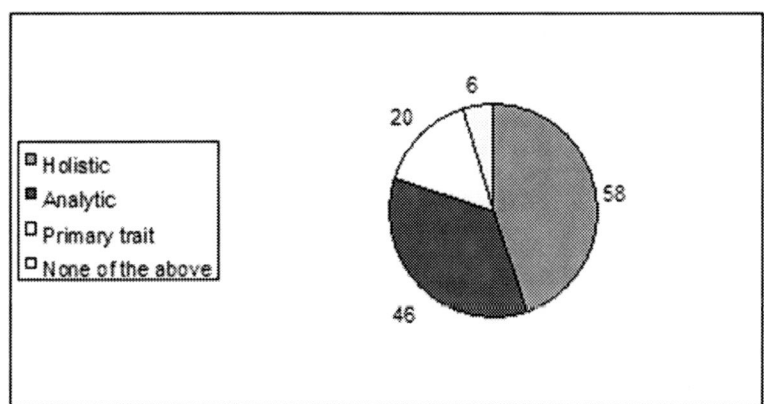

Figure 2 Types of scoring procedure used

Most of the lecturers (60%) have not heard about CBEM systems. However, it was encouraging to note that at least 40% of them have heard about CBEM systems. The results clearly show that most of the lecturers were not aware of the availability of CBEM systems.

The lecturers had a mixed opinion as to whether computers were able to mark essays effectively. It is interesting to note that although most of the lecturers (75%) did not believe that computers could mark essays effectively, 65% of them believed that computers were beneficial to them if computers can mark essays. This implies that to a certain extent, the lecturers believed that a computer was able to perform effectively in marking essays while some other aspects should be left to human markers.

The results from Table 1 show that most of the lecturers (57.5%) were of the opinion that a CBEM system should be able to indicate errors in essays. The next three important functions that a CBEM system should be able to perform were as follows: mark syntax and provide error statistics (47.5%); mark non-native speakers writing and produce a letter grade (42.5%); and mark organization of ideas (40.0%). A plausible reason for this expectation was that the lecturers believed that a computer can easily and effectively perform these functions while the rest of the functions should be performed by lecturers since these can best be carried out by humans.

Table 1. Lecturers' opinion of desirable functions that a CBEM system should provide

Functions that should be provided by a CBEM system	No. of respondents (percentage)
Indicate errors	46 (57.5 %)
Mark syntax	38 (47.5 %)
Provide error statistics	38 (47.5 %)
Mark non-native speakers writing	34 (42.5 %)
Produce letter grade	34 (42.5 %)
Mark organization of ideas	32 (40.0 %)
Mark surface features	30 (37.5 %)
Mark rhetorical structure	30 (37.5 %)
Mark topic content e.g. look at vocabulary	28 (35.0 %)
Give individual feedback	28 (35.0 %)
Mark holistically	28 (35.0 %)
Mark knowledge content e.g. look at semantics	26 (32.5 %)
Mark analytically	26 (32.5 %)
Mark according to disciplines	24 (30.0 %)

Other desirable functions (below 40% level) that a CBEM system should provide were mark surface features (37.5%), rhetorical structure (37.5%), topic content (35.0%), give individual feedback (35.0%), mark holistically (35.0%), mark knowledge content (32.5%) and mark analytically (32.5%). It was not surprising that to mark according to discipline (30.0%) was the least expected function for a computer to carry out because presumably humans can perform this more efficiently than a computer does.

The functions that were provided by available CBEM systems were compared against lecturers' expectation. It seems that none of the available CBEM systems satisfy all fourteen desirable functions. The system that came close to the lecturers' expectation at that time was *E-rater* where by it can perform nine out of the fourteen functions (Darus & Stapa, 2001). *Project Essay Grader* came next, as it was able to perform six functions. *Intelligent Essay Assessor* and *Markin 32*, both can perform four functions while *Methodical Assessment of Reports by Computer* only performed two functions. This implies that the currently available CBEM systems were not suitable for the Malaysian environment since they did not address the needs and expectations of Malaysian lecturers.

Contribution of the study

One significant contribution of this study to institutions of higher learning in Malaysia was that it indicated that there is a need to develop a new CBEM system for the Malaysian environment. The results of the study would be helpful for software engineers to develop a new CBEM system that satisfies Malaysian lecturers' expectations in marking essays.

Study 2: Investigating students' expectations of a CBEM system

The aim of Study 2 was to investigate the Malaysian students' expectations of a CBEM system. In particular the study addressed the following research questions:

1. In what areas would the students prefer to receive feedback?

2. Which level of feedback was most useful to students?

3. Were the available CBEM systems able to provide feedback in these areas of essay writing?

Methodology

A survey in the form of questionnaire was developed and given out to students who were currently studying at the Faculty of Language Studies, Universiti Kebangsaan Malaysia. The faculty was later restructured and now becomes the School of Language Studies and Linguistics, Faculty of Social Sciences and Humanities. The respondents were selected at random. A total number of 190 respondents participated in this study and the data collated were then analyzed.

The questionnaire consisted of 13 questions that were divided into four sections. The first section was about the respondents' background. The second section looked into their expectation of feedback from their instructors. The third and fourth section focused on the level of expected feedback and their opinions about CBEM systems respectively.

Background of respondents

Out of 190 students who participated in this study, 164 were female (86.3%) and 26 were male students (13.7%). The uneven distribution of female and male students was due to the fact that most of the students (more than 80%) in the faculty were female. In terms of area of specialization, 102 students (53.7%) specialized in language and education while 88 students (46.3%) in language studies only.

Results and discussion

Areas of feedback that were expected by the students are shown in Table 2. The four most important areas of feedback that students would expect to receive in essay writing were errors in the essay (84.2%), organization of ideas (65.3%), coherence of text (63.2%) and rhetorical structure (60.0%). A plausible reason for this expectation was that these were the most difficult areas in essay writing for non-native speakers. Thus, it is natural to expect that lecturers would focus more on these specific areas of essay writing. Other areas of feedback that were expected by respondents, at least at 50.0% level, were as follows: their writing in English, knowledge content, topic content, creativity and style of writing.

It was not surprising that syntax was the least expected feedback for these students (40.0%) because the availability of grammar checker in word processors has helped them in writing to a certain extent.

Table 2. Areas of feedback that students expect to receive

Areas of feedback	No of respondents (Percentage)
Errors in the essay	160 (84.2%)
Organization of ideas	124 (65.3%)
Coherence of text	120 (63.2%)
Rhetorical structure e.g. issue and argument	114 (60.0%)
Their writing in English	102 (53.7%)
Knowledge content e.g. by looking at semantics	100 (52.6%)
Topic content e.g. by looking at vocabulary	98 (51.6%)
Creativity	98 (51.6%)
Style of writing	96 (50.5%)
Syntax	76 (40.0%)

Table 3 indicates that most respondents were not interested in the results they obtained but rather they would like to know why their answers are correct or incorrect. This implies that the students were more interested in the higher level of diagnostic feedback as this type of feedback gave more insight to the strengths and weaknesses in their essays. Students at institutions of higher learning can normally use their higher order learning skills to produce correct answers once they are told why their answers are correct or incorrect. This explains the fact that not many respondents indicated the need for the other two types of feedback.

Table 3. Expected level of feedback that students look forward to receive

Level of feedback	Most useful 1 (%)	2 (%)	3 (%)	Least useful 4 (%)
Informs the results only	18.9	3.2	6.3	71.6
Informs why the answer is correct/incorrect	61.0	9.5	20	9.5
Informs how to produce a correct response	33.7	40	16.8	9.5
Informs what a correct response looks like	31.6	22.1	33.7	12.6

The functions that were provided by available CBEM systems were also compared against the students' expectation of a CBEM system. While some of these functions can be provided by these systems, none of the systems can provide all the nine areas of feedback as listed in Table 2. As far as level of feedback is concerned, we are not aware of any of the systems that are concerned with this issue.

Contribution of the study

There are two significant contributions of this study. The first contribution is that the result of the study can help lecturers to provide appropriate feedback when marking students' essays. The second contribution is that it also indicates that there is a need to develop a new CBEM system for the Malaysian environment. The software engineer of this new system can make use of the result of the study to develop a CBEM system that satisfies Malaysian students' expectations in marking essays, both in terms of the areas and levels of feedback. More detailed discussions on Study 2 can be found in (Darus, Hussin & Stapa, 2001).

Study 3: Experimenting a CBEM system in the Malaysian educational environment

The aim of Study 3 was to investigate whether feedback given by Criterion was useful to Malaysian students. In particular, the study addressed the following research questions:

1. In which areas did students find feedback given by Criterion useful to them?

2. Was feedback given by Criterion useful in revising their essays?

3. Was feedback given by Criterion more informative than feedback normally given by their lecturer?

Methodology

A total of 71 second-year students who were studying at the Universiti Kebangsaan Malaysia participated in this study. These students had taken a course entitled 'Advanced Writing' and 'Written Communication' in their first year. While doing the 'Written Communication' course, students had practiced writing in various forms of genres including persuasive writing.

Students were required to compose an essay of approximately 500 words in a 4-5 paragraphs format using the following prompt: Many adults become upset when young people break with the traditions of the past. Do you think that these adults are justified in reacting this way? Why or why not? Support your position with evidence from your own experience or the experience of people you know. This topic is persuasive in nature and it was chosen from a list of topics after consultation with the instructors of 'Advanced Writing' course. ETS Technologies provided a list of topics to choose from. The students were given two hours that was considered more than enough time to write this essay individually in the classroom in order to reduce the possibility of copying among students as compared to if this exercise was given as a take-home exercise. They were encouraged to discuss the topic with their classmates and use of dictionary was allowed. When the students had completed writing, their essays were collected.

The first author then typed all of these essays so that they were computer-readable, firstly in word documents and later converted to text documents. These essays were typed exactly as they were and no effort was taken to correct these essays. One had to access the ETS Technologies homepage (http://www.etstechnologies.com/criterion/student/) in order to submit these essays online by clicking on 'Complete an assignment' and entering an ID and password. The text documents were copied and pasted into the space given, one at a time. *Criterion* marked these essays by giving a score of 1-6. The highest score that a student could achieve was 6 and the lowest score was 1. Students' reports could be viewed by clicking on 'View my reports'.

The report and diagnostic feedback given by *Criterion* were printed and given back to the students. The students' original essay in the form of word document was also given back to them in the form of a soft copy in diskettes. Students were instructed to take into account the printed report as well as diagnostic feedback in revising their essays. After revision had taken place, students were required to save their revised essays in the diskette given. Students filled out a questionnaire and the diskette, as well as the printed report and diagnostic feedback were collected. The revised essays were then converted to text documents and resubmitted to *Criterion* for marking.

The questionnaire consisted of 13 questions that were divided into two sections. The first section comprised of six questions, enquiring about students' personal information as well as how often they wrote in English. Seven questions enquired about feedback from *Criterion* and this comprised the second section of the questionnaire.

Background of respondents

Out of 71 students who participated in this study, 46 students (65%) submitted their original essays, questionnaires and revised essays. Since the study needed to take into account all three materials, students who only submitted their questionnaires or original essays only were not considered. Altogether, 46 students' materials were taken into account; 42 females (91%) and 4 males (9%). The uneven distribution of female and male students was due to the fact that most of the students studying at the School of Language Studies and Linguistics were female.

Students apparently came from various geographical areas in Malaysia, with the highest percentage coming from the urban area (39%), followed by rural (32%) and sub-urban area (29%). The students were a mixture of ethnic groups, the largest being the Chinese (58.7%), followed by the Malays, Indians and others (41.3%). These students clearly wrote regularly in English (e.g., shopping list, e-mail and letters). 71.7 % wrote frequently and only 28.3 % wrote less frequently.

Results and discussion

Table 4 shows useful areas of feedback given by *Criterion*. The most useful area was feedback on errors in their essay (16.0%). The next useful feedback area was topic or knowledge content (14.0%). The lesser useful area of feedback was syntax (13.0%), style of writing and coherence of text (12.0%), rhetorical structure, organisation of ideas and creativity (11.0%). A previous study carried out by Darus et al. (2001) shows that four most important areas that students prefer to receive feedback in descending order were errors in their essay, organization of ideas, coherence of text and rhetorical structure. Other areas of feedback that students were interested in descending order were knowledge/topic content, creativity, style of writing and syntax. As far as *Criterion* feedback was concerned, it is clear from this study that students find feedback on errors most useful and, rhetorical structure, organization of ideas and creativity least useful. However, the values were very low and the range was between 11.0-16.0% only.

Table 4. Useful areas of Criterion feedback

Areas of feedback	Percentage (%)
Errors in essay	16.0
Topic or knowledge content	14.0
Syntax	13.0
Style of writing	12.0
Coherence of text	12.0
Rhetorical structure e.g. issue and argument	11.0
Organization of ideas	11.0
Creativity	11.0

Figure 3 shows usefulness of *Criterion* feedback in revising essay. Thirty-one students (67.39 %) found that *Criterion* feedback was only useful to some extent in revising their essay. Eleven students (23.91%) found *Criterion* feedback to be very useful, and three students (6.52%) found that it was not useful at all.

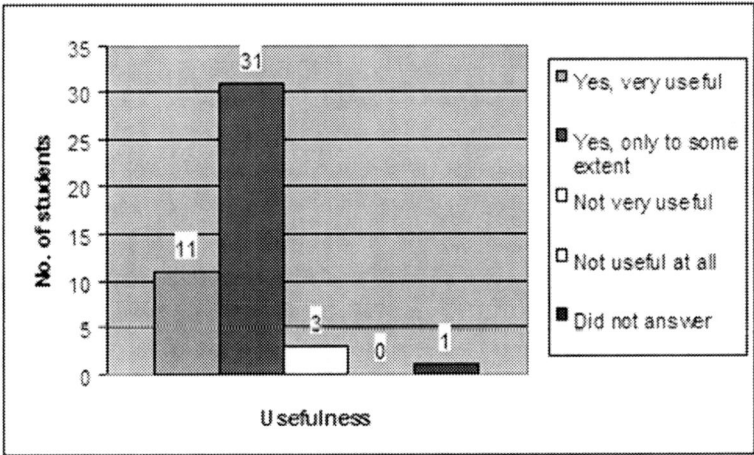

Figure 3 Usefulness of Criterion feedback in revising essay

Figure 4 shows the extent in which *Criterion* feedback was more informative. Fifteen students (32.6%) found that *Criterion* feedback was more informative while thirty students (65.2%) did not find that it was so.

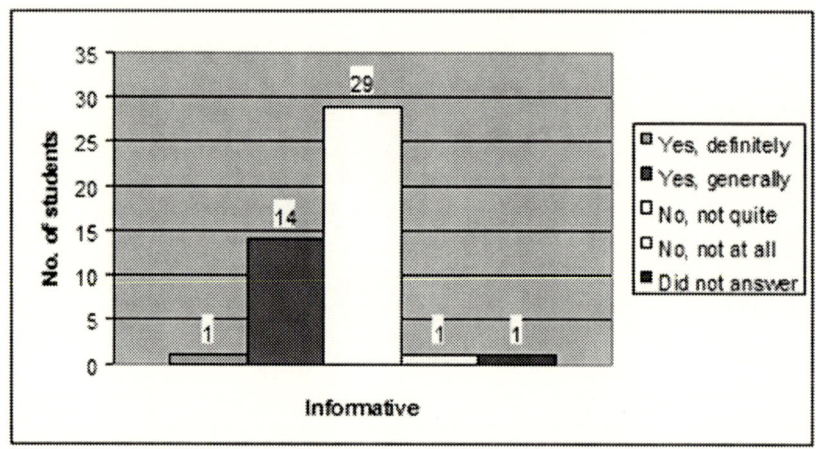

Figure 4 Criterion feedback was more informative

Table 5 shows the scores given by *Criterion* for students' original and revised essays. Out of 46 students who submitted their original essays, 3 students did not submit their revised essays. The score of their original and revised essays of majority of the students (83.71%) did not change, i.e. score 3 (13.95%), score 4 (41.86%), score 5 (25.58%) and score 6 (2.32%). 11.61 % of students were able to get a better score while 4.64% received a lower score after revision.

It seems that although students faithfully revised their essays based on the feedback given by *Criterion*, the revisions made were not able to significantly increase the score of revised essays for majority of the students. This could be due to the fact that feedback given by *Criterion* was not sufficient to enable students to do so. Apart from feedback on errors, topic or knowledge content and syntax that were useful to students, *Criterion* feedback in the other six areas namely style of writing, coherence of text, rhetorical structure, organization of ideas and creativity needs to be more fine tuned for these students so that they can benefit from feedback given.

Table 5. Criterion scores for original and revised essays

No. of students (%)	Score of original essay	Score of revised essay
6 (13.95)	3	3
1 (2.32)	3	4
1 (2.32)	3	6
18 (41.86)	4	4
2 (4.65)	4	5
1 (2.32)	5	4
11 (25.58)	5	5
1 (2.32)	5	6
1 (2.32)	6	5
1 (2.32)	6	6

Contribution of the study

The results of this study showed that *Criterion* feedback was useful to Malaysian students as ESL learners to a certain extent only and it was not that informative. It seems that *Criterion* was able to inform lecturers about students' base-line level of writing but it was not able to tutor the students to improve their writing. The results of this study further strengthened the fact that there is a need to develop a new CBEM system for ESL writing in Malaysian educational environments.

Conclusion

In the process of carrying out research in investigating Malaysian lecturers' claims that CBEM systems lack human touch and would not be able to give proper evaluation of Malaysian students' essays in ESL, we have investigated lecturers' and students' expectations of a CBEM system. We had also experimented the use of a CBEM system, namely *Criterion* in evaluating students' essays at tertiary level of education. The result of the study so far suggests that students' as well as lecturers' needs and expectations are not fully met by *Criterion*. In order for a CBEM system to be useful to the Malaysian educational environment, the software engineers need to develop a new CBEM system for the Malaysian ESL learners by taking into consideration the software requirement of lecturers and students as the end-users.

References

Ashwell, T. (2000). Patterns of teacher response to student writing in a multiple-draft composition classroom: Is content feedback followed by form feedback the best method. *Journal of Second Language Writing, 9*(3), 227-257.

Burstein, J., & Chodorow, M. (1999). Automated essay scoring for non-native English speakers. *Proceedings of the Association of Computational Linguistics 99 Workshop on Computer-Mediated Language Assessment and Evaluation of Natural Language Processing.* College Park, Maryland. Retrieved 2 May 2000, from the World Wide Web: http://www.ets.org/research/erater.html

Burstein, J., & Chodorow, M. (2002). Directions in automated essay analysis. In R. B. Kaplan (Ed.), *The Oxford handbook of applied linguistics* (pp. 487-497). New York: Oxford University Press.

Burstein, J., Kukich, K., Wolff, S., Lu, C., Chodorow, M., Braden-Harder, L., & Harris, M. D. (1998, August). *Automated scoring using a hybrid feature identification technique.* Paper presented at the Annual Meeting of the Association of Computational Linguistics, Montreal, Canada.

Burstein, J., Leacock, C., & Chodorow, M. (2003, August). Criterion[SM] online essay evaluation: *An application for automated evaluation of student essays.* Paper presented at the Fifteenth Annual Conference on Innovative Applications of Artificial Intelligence, Acapulco, Mexico.

Burstein, J., Wolff, S., & Lu, C. (1999). *Using lexical semantic techniques to classify free-responses*: Kluwer Academic Press.

Darus, S., Hussin, S., & Stapa, S. H. (2001). Students' expectations of a computer-based essay marking system. In J. Mukundan (Ed.), *Reflections, visions & dreams of practice: Selected papers from the IEC 2002 International Education Conference* (pp. 197-204). Kuala Lumpur, Malaysia: ICT Learning Sdn Bhd.

Darus, S., & Stapa, S. H. (2001). Lecturers' expectations of a computer-based essay marking system. *The English Teacher: Journal of the Malaysian English Language Teaching Association (MELTA), 30*(June), 47-56.

Darus, S., Stapa, S. H., Hussin, S., & Koo, Y. L. (2000). A survey of computer-based essay marking (CBEM) systems, *Proceedings of the International Conference on Education and ICT in the New Millennium* (pp. 519-529). Kuala Lumpur: Universiti Putra Malaysia.

Ferris, D., & Roberts, B. (2001). Error Feedback in L2 Writing Classes—How Explicit Does It Need to be? *Journal of Second Language Writing, 10,* 161-184.

Foltz, P. W., Kintsch, W., & Landauer, T. K. (1998). The measurement of textual coherence with latent semantic analysis. *Discourse Processes, 25*(2&3), 285-307.

Foltz, P. W., Laham, D., & Landauer, T. K. (1999). The intelligent essay assessor: Applications to educational technology. *Interactive Multimedia Electronic Journal of Computer-Enhanced Learning, 2*(4). Retrieved 8 February 2001, from the World Wide Web: http://imej.wfu.edu/articles/1999/2/04/index.asp

Gagne, R. M. (1985). *Conditions of learning* (3rd Ed.). New York: CBS College Publishing.

Holmes, M. (1996). Marking student work on the computer. *The Internet TESL Journal, II*(9), 6.

Krajka, J. (2002). Correcting student work with the computer—using dedicated software and a word processor. *Teaching English with Technology: A Journal for Teachers of English, 2*(4).

Ley, K. (1999). Providing feedback to distant students. *Campus-Wide Information Systems, 16*(2), 63-69.

Marshall, S., & Barron, C. (1987). MARC—Methodical Assessment of Reports by Computer. *System, 15*(2), 161-167.

Mory, E. H. (1996). Feedback research. In D. H. Jonassen (Ed.), *Handbook of Research for Educational Communications and Technology* (pp. 919-956). New York: Macmillan.

Page, E. B. (1996). *Project Essay Grade and writing traits: Qualitative and quantitative combined?* NCME Symposium. New York. Retrieved 11 April 2000, from the World Wide Web: http://134.68.49.185/pegdemo/ref/Qual&Qual-b96.htm

Page, E. B., & Peterson, N. C. (1995). The computer moves into essay grading: Updating the ancient test. *Phi Delta Kappan, 76*(7), 561-565.

Page, E. B., & Truman, D. L. (1994, November). *A teacher's helper: Proposed use of project essay grade for the English classroom.* Paper presented at the Annual Meeting of the South Atlantic Modern Language Association, Baltimore.

Shermis, M. D., Mzumara, H. R., Olson, J., & Harrington, S. (2001). On-line grading of student essays: PEG goes on the World Wide Web. *Assessment & Evaluation in Higher Education, 26*(3), 247-259.

Silva, T. (1990). Second language composition instruction: Developments, issues, and directions in ESL. In B. Kroll (Ed.), *Second language writing: Research insights for the classroom* (pp. 11-23). New York: Cambridge University Press.

Smith, P., & Ragan, T. (1992). *Instructional design.* New York: Merrill.

Walvoord, B. E., & Anderson, V. J. (1998). *Effective grading: A tool for learning and assessment.* San Francisco, California: Jossey-Bass.

White, E. M. (1998). *Teaching & assessing writing: Recent advances in understanding, evaluating and improving student performance* (2nd Ed.). Portland, Maine: Calendar Islands Publishers.

Wolfe, M., Schreiner, M., Rehder, B., Laham, D., Foltz, P. W., Kintsch, W., & Landaeur, T. K. (1998). Learning from text: Matching readers and texts by Latent Semantic Analysis. *Discourse Processes, 25*(2&3), 309-336.

0-595-33126-2

Printed in the United States
219230BV00003B/59/A